What's up
with your

handshake?

What's up
with your

handshake?

Using the Secrets of
Strategic Communication and

Soft Skills to **Win**

MARK JEFFRIES

www.markjeffries.com

What's Up with Your Handshake?
by Mark Jeffries
www.markjeffries.com

First published in the United Kingdom in 2008 by Mark Jeffries
c/o Redford & Co,
64 Baker Street,
London, W1U 7GB,
United Kingdom

A catalogue record for this book is available from the British Library.

ISBN 978-0-9558825-0-0

Set in Bembo and Gill Sans
Printed and bound in Great Britain by
Hill and Garwood, Watford, Hertfordshire, United Kingdom.

Contents

Introduction

How often do you sit back at your desk, stare out of the window, sigh and consider where you should be at this point in your life? Where do those thoughts take you? The executive offices on the top floor? Turning left to your first-class bed on that overnight flight? Winning "sales rep of the year"? Running your own successful business? Banking a cheque that actually *has* a figure in the "hundreds of thousands" box? Signing yet another multimillion–dollar deal?

You're doing well, you have all the right ambitions, but maybe those huge "wins" only happen to other people, right? Do those people possess some secret magical abilities or fabulous good luck? The reality is that their continued success is a lot closer to you than you might imagine.

All of those wonderful things and more are available to everyone, and we have far greater control over our destinies than we think. Those people – the industry leaders, the deal-makers, the ones living it up in first class, the elite players running businesses worth billions of dollars, the ones who love their jobs and lives – all have an essential element to their characters which, while crucial, is not always that obvious. But it's there and it's doing most of the work.

Soft skills' or "strategic communication" is the rare and very valuable ability to connect, influence others, successfully pitch ideas and persuade people that they not only want you but that they actually *need* you as well. In other words – in addition to their skills and knowledge – those winners

have all used their ability to strategically communicate their way to the top. Sounds like hypnotic magic but, I can assure you, it is pretty simple and there for anyone to exploit.

The good news is you don't need wildly staring eyes to succeed. There's no "magic" or chicanery involved; nor do the skills you are about to learn require hours of study, or subscription to a sweeping new life philosophy. I am reluctant to describe them as "common sense" – after all, if they were common, everyone would be using them. But they are deceptively simple, wonderfully advantageous and everyone really *can* develop them.

What if the business world isn't your main concern? Don't worry if you are not aspiring to be the next Richard Branson, Steve Jobs or Bill Gates! These skills can be applied equally well to *any* social situation that involves interaction with other people, whether it be going on a first date (and wanting to secure a second), attending a party on your own, addressing a community meeting, being interviewed for a new job or resolving a family dispute. Regardless of the scale of the changes you would like to achieve, whether you are active in business or not, these skills will enhance your life.

WHAT ARE SOFT SKILLS?

This is the first question that everyone asks me! In the first instance, it is perhaps easier to define them by what they are *not*. For example, what are *hard* skills? For a software developer, it's the ability to write brilliant code; for an artist it is the ability to mix colours and wield a paintbrush; for an accountant it is an aptitude for figures and sums; for a criminal lawyer it is a knowledge of legal practice and an ability to argue a case; in business it's seeing an opportunity and creating a method to take a *profit*. Hard skills are thus all those skills and qualifications that enable you to practise your specific profession.

Soft skills, on the other hand, are far more ephemeral and wide-ranging. "Soft skills" is an umbrella term for anything that enables you to influence others, to pitch ideas successfully and to persuade people that they not only want you, but *need* you as well. *Fortune* magazine recently reported that the major American business schools, including Wharton,

Chicago and Berkeley Haas, have all started emphasizing "soft skills". In a 2007 speech to MIT, former CEO of GE, Jack Welch, said "Just concentrate on networking" – the ultimate soft skill. *CIO* magazine said, "It is not easy to fully appreciate the importance of soft skills". Workforce.com wrote in April 2007 that, following a survey, they found that "67% of hiring managers say they would hire an applicant with strong 'soft' skills, even if their technical skills were lacking".

"Soft skills" apply to all aspects of presentation (from your dress code and grooming to the design of your letterhead), body language (both your own and your ability to interpret others'), effective greeting and communication skills, your use of language and your ability to read the needs and emotions of others. You are aiming to introduce your promise and potential – all those things that set you apart and present you as *better* than everyone else.

Executed well, soft skills will get people to do and think what you want without them realizing what you are up to. It's about gently influencing people to come round to your way of thinking while getting them to imagine that they have come to this conclusion on their own. You are subtly manipulating the way others perceive you. In each situation, you need people to see you in one light or another; you will become a "social chameleon". Only by adapting to a current situation can you be truly successful in all that you do.

Every scenario will call for a different approach. In front of a CEO, you will need to appear confident, competent and in control – someone whose contribution directly adds to the bottom line. In front of a potential lover, you are now a listener – you convey interest, passion and humour. With a new client, you become inspirational and motivating – you help them to visualize how you are going to be of benefit to them. Your confidence is set at just the right level to inspire confidence in them; in many ways, you even start to appear just like them – creating a perfect match.

WHERE IT ALL STARTED...

So far you might say I've been doing something of a "hard sell" – trying to convince you that soft skills are indispensable to your life and situation! Let me step aside from that for a moment and tell you a bit about myself.

That might be my most effective sales tool of all – telling you how these soft skills have transformed my *own* life.

School has a lot to answer for. I went to a decent school in the Liverpool area of England. It wasn't all bad, but my one, overriding memory is the sense of failure that came with my second-rate exam results. I achieved mediocre passes in only five subjects at O- (Ordinary) Level (these are exams taken in England at the age of 16, usually in 8–12 subjects); hardly promising. More ominously, I secured an outright "Fail" in Spoken English. These were certainly not the promising signs of someone destined, as it turned out, for a life in broadcasting and public speaking! This very fact, however, is a clear indication that academic exam results are not the sole barometer of an individual's potential or talents. I have often wondered just how many people attending my seminars – or reading this book – have felt pigeon-holed and limited their aspirations as a result of similar early "failures".

How, then, did I transform myself from this unpromising teenager to an adult with a successful, fulfilling business in the very field in which I was deemed most unsuited?

Dealing with that kind of bitter disappointment became, in fact, the most important thing that my school years could have taught me. Failure is never the end – just another bend in the winding road to success. Two things are certain. *No one* fails permanently, and *everyone* possesses the ability to succeed. Failure is a crucial part of our individual learning curve. The sting of rejection can point us towards a more successful direction. Every lesson learned strengthens our hand. This may explain what I call the "Fabulous Failure Phenomenon".

HOW THE MIGHTY FALL

The following is based purely on personal experience and anecdotal evidence – I don't claim for a minute that it is the evidence of a controlled scientific survey. Nevertheless, I am sure there is enough core truth in the following stories that you *will* recognize.

I have discovered that those school companions of mine who were great-looking, naturally talented and universally popular often fell on hard times later in life. It seems that things came to them so easily early on that it soon became second nature to coast through studies and life – they lived a "charmed" life. These teenage stars received all the attention and accolades, and concluded that it was going to be this easy for ever. They acquired a sense of entitlement and complacency – and stopped making an effort. They experienced no failures or setbacks, and thus learned few lessons.

Fast-forward 10 years and the balance had shifted. As time went on, through laziness or complacency, these high achievers often lost their edge or charisma. Suddenly they were placed in the far more competitive environment of university, business and "real life", and they were no longer exceptional. They were now competing against the best from every high school, business school, college and university in the land. Instead of two or three rivals, they now had two or three thousand. Unless they had something extra to set themselves apart, they really began to appear quite ordinary. Moreover, because they had never experienced such a setback before, the shock was often enough to undo them. Many sank and did not swim.

Conversely, some of those people who previously had not been blessed with early irresistibility, some of those for whom success was often difficult or even impossible to achieve, those who had faced social rejection, started to accelerate ahead. Driven by the lessons of previous failures and a desire to catch up and succeed, those quiet and unassuming students grew into more confident, often more successful people. Compelled to be more resourceful and hard-working, their growing wit and confidence started to tilt the scales in their favour.

Of course, there are many exceptions to the "Fabulous Failure Phenomenon" – plenty of high achievers remain just that. Nevertheless, I have come across it now so often in my work that I am sure you, too, can think of someone from school who has not fulfilled their promise. Conversely, many low achievers also remain just that. A key factor in the success of those who go on to exceed expectations, however, is that they did not give up. Early setbacks made them only more determined to succeed. They did not become resigned to mediocrity and vaguely stare at their dreams from a distance. So, from this point on, like many great leaders, you should view failure as a great opportunity to learn. I knew one charismatic salesman at a global IT firm who would celebrate every knock-back by announcing that he was one step closer to success. He was right – and ended up making a fortune.

BUY LOW, SELL HIGH

Thankfully, I chose not to give up. But with little in the way of academic achievement to carry me through, I had to rely upon something else. I soon discovered this to be of far more value than an A-grade in Latin – my ability to communicate strategically.

My first job as a stockbroker for Merrill Lynch in London all came about through my, at the time, unwitting use of soft skills. Knowing that I would have a better chance of getting a job on the trading desk if I already worked within the company, I got myself a temporary data-entry job. I didn't have a clue what the information was that I was so busy inputting, or where it was going. I knew that I turned up every day and sat there like one of those well-trained chimpanzees that you can see on YouTube.

In my lunch breaks I accessed the other floors of this huge office complex, discovered who was in charge of what and decided where I most wanted to be. After this illicit research was complete, it was simply a matter of picking up the internal phone at the close of trading, and dialling the relevant extension to speak to the boss of the desk I had chosen – London traded options.

The upshot of this first effort at engineering a situation to suit myself was that I was offered a job on the trading desk as an assistant. Lowly, yes, but it was a good start. It was particularly satisfying that I had been successful in bypassing all the other contenders who were phoning in from the cold outside world, with not a chance of getting through to the boss!

On my first morning, I arrived bright and early, riding high, flush with enthusiasm and ready for my glittering new career. But, as the elevator doors opened, I witnessed what could only be described as the end of the world and, with it, the shattering of all my dreams and ambitions. My first day in my new job happened to be 19 October 1987 – Black Monday – the biggest stock-market crash for decades.

As I watched brokers and traders running around in panic, while others sat motionless with their heads in their hands in a state of shock, I concluded that it was a huge conspiracy directed against me. I phoned my mother. *"It's all over"*, I said. *"I'm going to need my bedroom back."*

Thankfully, I never did have to take up my parents' offer of my old room back and a job in the local school-outfitters shop (this had been a constant threat whenever I had become lax about my homework and exam results while growing up). This entire experience was truly the founding of my soft-skills revolution. Yes, that's right – it took the sight of grown men crying and the threat of having to measure up bratty kids for their school uniforms to create the communications consultancy that I now proudly run.

WE ARE *ALL* IN SALES

The minute you step out of the door every morning, you are being judged. We judge each other all the time. People are looking at you, listening to you, weighing you up and deciding whether to "buy" into you as a person or not.

Imagine someone offering you a big contract, a pay rise or a new job. They look at your résumé; they check the facts – your hard skills – but they also look at *you*. They listen to your words, watch your gestures, evaluate your looks, they wonder if you will fit in with their team, whether people will like you – if you're worth it. They are weighing up how attractive you are to their needs, how closely you match the opening they have. Regardless of your previous track record, you can never afford to become complacent. You are relentlessly "selling" yourself, and people around you are continually deciding whether to "buy" you or not.

Whether you are a doctor recommending one course of treatment over another, a pilot explaining an aircraft delay to disgruntled passengers, a solutions integrator suggesting a course of action, a tax expert advising a particular financial approach, a marketer with a creative plan, or a consultant with a proposal, you are selling – both your ideas and yourself.

For those millions of people who do not work directly in sales, this idea is often a hard one to swallow; they dismiss it as irrelevant to them, and it is often lost or forgotten. But this idea can often make the difference,

for example, between the talented artist who for ever remains the impoverished amateur and the one who secures gallery space and receives attention and commissions – actually making money from their talent.

It is soft skills that make this difference. The beauty is that what your soft skills offer – information, compliments, contacts, confidence, ideas and inspiration – cost you nothing, but can *earn* you so much (better jobs, bigger contracts, greater fulfilment).

Look at these two statements, both issued during a job interview:

STATEMENT 1	STATEMENT 2
"I would really like to work here. I am ambitious and know that I will be successful."	"I could really add to your bottom line. If you bring me into your organization, we could work together and achieve some amazing goals."

What's wrong with Statement 1? After all, it demonstrates plenty of enthusiasm and confidence. But look again. It is a statement of pure self-interest, about the speaker's goals, what they will take – not what they will give. Now look at Statement 2. While the tone still conveys confidence and enthusiasm, the words are offering an attractive shared goal, by creating the visualization of the person's presence in the organization. The speaker is offering something before, very subtly, asking for the job.

We sell most effectively when we make something sound more attractive. I call this "menu theory". Think of a restaurant menu; you would be far more interested in "Tarragon roasted duck breast on a creamy leek mash" than "Bits of dead bird on some vegetables". Clearly this is an oversimplified example, but it illustrates my point. The clear and effective use of language and other presentation skills wins you trust and earns you respect – it clinches the sale.

IMAGE AND PRESENTATION

We live in an image-conscious age. The dozens of reality and "make-over" TV shows – whether they're making over your dress sense or your home décor – bear testimony to this. We ignore the importance of image and presentation at our peril. The world is just too competitive to hope that someone will see our innate talent and look beyond the untrimmed hair and multiple creases on the suit.

It's no good having a fantastic idea or product if it is not presented at its best. You would not hang the *Mona Lisa* in a splintered frame in a dimly lit, musty room with the paint peeling off the walls. Many people would lack the perception to notice the painting itself and would just want to get out of there as quickly as possible. When it comes to selling your home, again, presentation is key. Similarly, many would-be buyers lack the imagination to see the potential of a property and are put off by too much clutter or strong colour. Even though they may *know* a room measures 14ft by 16ft, if it *feels* cluttered and dark, they mentally register the room as small. Transform the room with a lick of white paint and less furniture, and, bingo, house sold. Again, it is a matter of perception, influencing how other people perceive what you have to sell.

Exactly the same principle is at work with you, the person. Soft skills are the tool, but don't forget the tool handler – you. Look at yourself. Ask yourself what people may think about you. What sort of first impression do you make? If you are the brand, how strong is your presentation, how attractive is your "label"? The way you walk, the clothes you wear, the way you talk, all are crucial in delivering your message successfully.

An effective test is to forget what people say to your face; instead, ask yourself what they say once you have left the room. Have you left a positive impression or, once you have closed the door behind you, are they sniggering and scoffing? It's difficult to know. There are ways to be sure. One is the approach that the *Seinfeld* character George Costanza employed. He left a tape recorder running in his briefcase, made a huge scene about having to leave and "accidentally" left the briefcase in the conference room with his colleagues. He didn't like what he heard!

I would certainly advise you against resorting to such tactics. Instead, I recommend you follow the ideas in this book. You will learn how to influence those around you so that they form very positive opinions of who you are and what you stand for. You will become so proficient at reading the way people respond to you that, when you finally do leave the room, you will have the quiet confidence of someone who knows exactly what people will be saying. And it will all be good!

In choosing the title for this book I have used the handshake as a metaphor for soft skills as a whole. But the handshake part of our presentation is incredibly important in itself. I know, we have all been shaking hands for a long time .... Seriously, how much more can there be to it? But, incredibly, so very many people get this stage of first-impression-making horribly wrong, you'd think it was as difficult to master as playing a piano blindfold with no lessons and the lid closed. Later in the book, you will find out if you are getting it right and how you can ensure that this crucial moment helps you to maximize your impact on new contacts.

TINY DIFFERENTIATORS

We all have a comparative effectiveness score, and every month, every week, every day it always starts at the same point – 50%. That means that compared to everyone else in our "sector" (our

YOUR COMPARATIVE EFFECTIVENESS SCORE – 50%

competitors offering similar product, similar price, similar contribution) we are no better and no worse. We all get the 50% score.

As time goes on, however, and your ability to sprinkle effective soft skills, strategic communication and confident presentation into your interactions with others improves, your score has the potential to rise. Naturally if you get these things wrong, the score can also fall. Fifty per cent simply represents the starting line. At this number you are neither in control of a situation nor has it slipped out of your control. A figure of 50.1% and upwards puts you comparatively in control; 49.9% and lower and you are losing it! By using the ideas in this book you will have the best chance to keep your effectiveness score above 50% – always in control and always successful.

I first devised this method of understanding one's effectiveness through a client, a New York law firm. It had unexpectedly just won a big account worth something in the region of $2 million. I was working with the firm's partners on another new project and wanted to know why they thought they had been able to clinch this one. What was it about their pitch that had convinced the client – a huge utility firm – to place the business in the hands of this law firm?

The senior partner couldn't put his finger on it, so went back to the client and asked why his firm had been awarded the business. The client made a simple but hugely insightful comment. He said:

"To us, you lawyers all come over the same. You all look the same, offer the same service at the same price across the same timescale – all very capable, well educated and with impeccable backgrounds. However, you guys came along and were just that little bit different. You caught our eye; we all seemed to get on. I remember talking about how bad Yankee pitching had become with your project finance guy and we decided that if we had to spend six months 'in the trenches' with a firm on this big job, we'd rather it was you than someone else. We liked you."

The firm won a $2-million job based on likeability? On a casual discussion about baseball?! Yes, it had. Likeability had become its differentiator. It had propelled the firm above the 50% line and distinguished it from all the other perfectly capable law firms that remained stuck at the start.

This is just one example, of course. On any given deal or interaction, the differentiator could be anything, and can be different each time. Depending on the product or skills set you are selling, however, it may be fairly consistent. Perhaps you have some expertise or specialist knowledge that your competitors lack. Whatever it is, remember that it can also be the small, imperceptible, almost subconscious things that can make all the difference.

PAYBACK

I believe that most of us are fundamentally good, and that it is just real life – pressure of a deadline, money worries, stress and tiredness, and so forth – that get in the way. We all have a sense of balance, justice and decency. Admittedly, this sense is less active in some people than others, but it is there, and it can work very much in your favour if you know how to draw upon it.

Our need to pay back acts of generosity and kindness is strong. We are happy to tip great service in restaurants; we feel indebted when a friend helps us out of trouble or when we are given an unexpectedly generous gift. Someone picking up something you dropped, a stranger helping you when you're struggling with heavy luggage, a contact putting in a good word for you – all these things put a smile on our faces and make us feel right with the world. These are all acts of generosity that deserve, in our human way of trying to make everything balance and round off nicely, to be paid back.

Just to illustrate how much we *need* payback, think how it feels when you don't get the payback you think you deserve. For example, let's say you're driving to work and pull in behind a parked car to let the oncoming traffic pass. As a basic courtesy, you do expect the passing driver to raise his hand in acknowledgement. But when they don't, when they determinedly ignore you and drive on past, while taking advantage of your generosity … you are enraged!! Indignation and resentment can boil up, and it can put you in a bad mood for the rest of the day. As a payback, we *needed* that wave!

Deliver acts of kindness and generosity both in business and in life, and your targets will feel the need to pay you back. This dynamic of reciprocity is one that you can take advantage of in all your business and social interactions, and I will be showing you how to do this in the first chapter.

THE SOFT-SKILLS MIND-SET

Aside from a determination to fulfil your potential, self-belief is important. I expect many of you already possess this, and are confident that you have something good to offer. But you might well have a problem convincing other people of this. Remember those two sample statements? One was all about *"what I can get"*; the other was all about *"what I can offer"*. Most people approach a pitch situation asking, *"How can I get what I want?"* Just imagine how much more successful you can be once you shift your whole mind-set and approach truly to reflect *"What can I really do for them?"*

We all have the power to improve ourselves and influence others. In every encounter you have with someone from whom you want something, you need to make yourself appealing – you are the brand. The smartest players in this game are those who convince their "target" that *they* want and need *you*.

You will be stunned at what you can achieve. From now on, instead of skirting around a prize target – such as your CEO, a potential client or crucial promotion – feeling that it's probably best to wait or that you simply aren't worthy enough, you'll be making a direct beeline for that golden opportunity. After reading this book, you'll *know* you can do it and you'll be confident that you know *how* to deliver it.

This book will show you how to apply soft skills in every possible business and social situation: from innovative networking ideas to the etiquette of the boardroom; from revealing your "elevator pitch" to winning the business; from proposing your idea to negotiating the deal; from maximizing your payback to understanding the powerful effects of your voice and tone; from the science of "techniquette" to the art of the perfect handshake. This book is your ultimate guide to the little things that make a huge difference, bringing you success at every turn.

There is no luck involved in this sort of success: it involves the right preparation meeting with the right opportunity. Now you can control both. This book will arm you with the best practice tailored to your individual needs that will:

- earn you that fortune
- win you that new business
- and convince others that you have what it takes.

BEFORE WE MOVE ON TO THE EXCITING STUFF THERE ARE THREE KEY THEMES I REALLY WANT YOU TO BEAR IN MIND:

1   We are all in sales (whether we like it or not).

2   Tiny differentiators make the big difference.

3   We feel the need to pay back acts of generosity.

CHAPTER 1

The Soft-Skills Tool Kit

At the end of the Introduction, I introduced the concepts of "likeability" and "payback" – a core instinct that drives most people to repay kindness and generosity. Delivering kindness and generosity is a great way of doing business. It uses our natural human tendencies and emotions, and converts them into an advantageous and positive networked connection. We are now going to look at this in more detail and also at how you can make this dynamic work to your advantage through the effective use of soft skills.

LIKEABILITY

There are probably very few people, if any, we truly hate. But in every walk of life and line of business we encounter people we find it difficult to like: the sales guy aggressively pushing a sale on a reluctant customer; a colleague talking about you behind your back; friends who never listen; a call-centre operative who clearly doesn't care. The list could go on for ever.

After all, it's a competitive world out there. On those occasions when you are on the receiving end of an act of kindness or generosity, they certainly make a difference. Sadly, today they seem so rare that they can often pull you up short in astonishment at what has just happened.

It's so easy to be brusque, angry and impatient, but it never leaves you or anyone else feeling good. I really want to encourage you to introduce spontaneous acts of kindness – paying someone a compliment; taking the time to ask how the receptionist (whom you may usually ignore) is – into your day-to-day life. Don't be alarmed: this book is not a covert course on sainthood. I want you to develop this aspect of all your interactions with other people because it really can pay dividends in business.

Many companies spend millions of dollars training salespeople to be salespeople, which – no offence – is a bit like training a fish to swim. What they should be doing is *coaching* salespeople to connect and relate to their potential customers; to exercise their soft skills.

It's on old saying, but "people buy people". More specifically, people buy likeable people who are similar to themselves and whose company they enjoy and whose generosity they appreciate. Whatever line of business you are in, the ability to connect with a client or potential customer first as a person – to get them to like you, no matter how brief or superficial the encounter – will nearly always make the difference that leads to a successful outcome.

COMFORT

Just how do you go about getting people to like you? In a quick sales call, you need to rely on good manners and a pleasant tone of voice (something we shall be exploring in a later chapter). In a more long-term negotiation – wooing a new client for example – there are more factors to draw upon.

Think about your friends, the people whom you like and whom like you. You probably have lots in common, shared hobbies and interests and experiences. The simple truth is we are most comfortable when we are with people who are like us. You can use this to your advantage in business. In the world of soft skills, making yourself similar to your targets always pays off.

Try wherever possible to adopt the views, tastes and interests of your target. Do this at a slow and steady pace, and before long you will have them feeling comfortable in your company, trusting you as a colleague and seeing you as a friend. Naturally, if your current clients like you and find you easy to work with, they are far more likely to refer you to their contacts who, in turn, could become your new clients.

GENEROSITY AND THE DOG

We already oil the wheels of business with acts of generosity (albeit with an ulterior motive – winning or retaining the business of our clients), such as taking them out to dinner or sending them a hamper at Christmas. We all do it, and it tends to work OK. The dinner meeting will often produce a result, but not always. It does not set you apart because everyone else does it, too. You have not given yourself the advantage of having delivered a *"differentiator of generosity"* (DOG).

A DOG is something that you should constantly strive to deliver. Here is a good example of an effective DOG. Your potential client is a keen tennis player, so you agree to set up and pay for a game between the two of you. As a surprise, however, you have arranged for a former regional tennis champion to come along and offer you both some great tips. He will obviously concentrate on your potential client, who will be left feeling great and having received one hell of a DOG from you. Far more memorable and effective than dinner for two at the Taj Mahal restaurant. The result?: potential payback on a big scale (see below).

It's worth pointing out that as compliance and business behaviours become ever more closely monitored, the nature of these acts of "generosity" must be very carefully considered. The subtler, smarter and more tailored to the individual target they are, the fewer problems you will have.

Perhaps all this sounds like cynical manipulation – that I am suggesting that you give *only* in order to get something back. This is not the case. The sort of generosity and proactivity I am talking about will work only if it is appropriate to the person and situation, and if it appears spontaneous and sincere. It is not a subtle form of bribery to get what you want! After all, the payback may be a long time in coming to you, and perhaps not in a form you can predict. Furthermore, if these acts are inappropriate or disproportionate, they can make people feel uncomfortable and can arouse suspicion – "Hmm, what's he after?"

So we are not taking about complicated and long-thought-out strategies of bribery and manipulation. Rather, just basic acts of human kindness, a friendly disposition, an awareness of others. In all our relationships and social interactions, we are probably aware of the "give and take", even if only on a subconscious level. Now all I am asking you to do is to bring this dynamic to the forefront of your thinking. All you have to do is perform that act of generosity to create a "payback credit" – that unofficial "I owe you". Soon you will have created a "payback bank account" brimming with potential help, guidance, referrals and recommendations, ideas and future business from those to whom you are good.

The great news is that you can run this account at a healthy profit. The acts of generosity, kindness and consideration that you offer to others needn't cost much at all in terms of cash or time, but the payback credit is real and positive.

(Examples of the sort of things I'm talking about, more of which can be found in chapter 8, could include: interesting ideas, links to cool or useful websites, recommendations of movies, restaurants, people or companies – all easy and free to deliver, but all of which demonstrate thought and care.)

BUILDING UP PAYBACK CREDITS

So, how can we best build up this account full of payback credits? The most effective way to do this is by getting to know your intended target well. You must make it your business to learn about their likes and dislikes, their habits, their family members, their hobbies, sports and passions. Only once armed with this knowledge can you make a gesture with meaning, something that is appropriate to them.

Remember, you aren't simply going out, buying an expensive item and dispatching it as a bribe. You are demonstrating that you really listen, care and remember what you have been told. You are showing yourself to be a good person with whom to be associated. Let's have a look at a couple of examples.

One client of mine enjoys doing business with me and obviously wants to continue the association. She knows that I am a total foodie, I love cool new restaurants and that I adore cooking. Every so often I receive a courier package from her. It will usually contain some fabulous small food item, often bought from the wonderful bustling Ferry Building food market in San Francisco. It's always stuff that I love, and I am always bowled over by how surprising and appropriate the item is. I always get straight back in touch with my thanks.

Her thoughtfulness means that I am now automatically predisposed to helping her in return. If she said to me, *"Mark, I need a favour – I want you to come and address this group but my budget is so tight. Could you help me out?"* I would do it in a flash. Those little food items are one part of the payback credit, but far more powerful is the fact that she took the trouble to get to know me. That effort, the apparent care and interest, is what I want to reward.

I was chatting to a senior analyst at an event in Las Vegas recently, and he was waxing lyrical about Apple's new iPhone – how cool it was and how he wanted one. Now, I'm hardly going to go out and buy him one – that would be wholly inappropriate. But I do want to develop a positive relationship with this well-connected executive. How could I use this seemingly trivial bit of chit-chat to my advantage?

I spent five minutes hunting for some cool video clips of new iPhones on YouTube. I sent him an email with the links embedded, and he loved it. He immediately replied, thanked me and committed to staying in touch, and – great anchor point – in my reply, I made him promise to let me know when he had finally bought one.

Five networking soft-skills points were earned here:

1 I put myself on his radar and reminded him who I was.

2 I demonstrated that I had remembered what he had said.

3 I had given him something – cool on-line content, saving him search time.

4 I had associated myself with something he really liked – the iPhone.

5 I created an anchor point to encourage further contact.

Clearly, if he ever reads this book, he'll conclude that I'm a cynical dealer in soft skills and that the whole thing was a ruse – but it wasn't, honest!

PAYBACK ETIQUETTE – CASHING IN YOUR CREDITS

The etiquette of cashing in all of these valuable payback credits is delicate. There has to be some payback at least some of the time, or you end up simply being a charity, always giving things out and getting nothing in return. Let's not forget: this is business.

You clearly invalidate a payback credit if you have to remind someone of what you did. Don't use it to hold a gun to someone's head. *"Hey, Frank, don't forget that I got you tickets to that ball game. I really expect your help here."* **Payback value = 0.**

However, having already delivered your act of kindness, you can assume, reasonably enough, that your target is at least aware that a debt is owed. *"Hey, Frank, if you have a chance I would be really grateful for a bit of assistance on something. Call me back when you get a moment."* **Payback value = 1.**

Yes, you are reliant on someone's memory. So it is important to try to cash in your credit within a reasonably short amount of time. You should also ensure that whatever you did to create that credit was memorable in some way. Holding the door open for someone on the way into the office on a rainy Monday morning is not sufficient credit to ask someone to pull an all-nighter helping you to finish a report!

You get only one or two chances to be paid back. Even if you flew someone's entire family to Aspen to go skiing, you can milk this situation only once or twice – maximum. So choose your paybacks carefully.

USEFUL PHRASES TO INITIATE PAYBACK

Never *assume* that you will get anything back. Don't act as if you're now entitled to make demands of other people. When you do politely ask for something, however, you will be activating a very human instinct to pay you back.

Subtlety is the order of the day. Here are some sample phrases that demonstrate the right sort of tone to take:

"It's probably a lot to ask ..."
"I know you're very busy but ..."

"I'm sure this is a little unusual ..."
"I wouldn't usually ask but ..."
"I would love your opinion on ..."
 "Your guidance on this opportunity would be great."
"Can you think of someone who could ...?"

Note that many of these phrases also contain a subtle compliment to the target's skills and expertise – most people welcome the opportunity to show off a little. Try to avoid asking for "help" or, worse, asking for "a minute of their time" – this makes you sound too much like a door-to-door salesman!

Sometimes the most effective way to get the payback you want is to ask for it indirectly – again, the subtle approach. Let's say, for example, you want some help creating some really special graphics for a presentation. And let's just say you are owed some payback from the office computer whizz. If you simply went and asked them for their input outright, they could say yes, but they could also give you an outright *"No"*. Now look at the alternative: *"Could you think of someone who could ...?"* If payback is working efficiently and you've proven yourself in the past, their gut reaction should be, *"Yes, me! Don't worry about this. Let me take care of it for you."* If they don't react like this, they can still at least answer your original question and refer you to someone else who can help you.

Needless to say, the payback credit system is just one weapon in your arsenal of soft skills and should be used sparingly. If your target is discovering baskets of flowers, baseballs signed by his favourite team, puppies in boxes and dancing girls on his doorstep every day, you are probably going too far!

KEEP YOURSELF ON THE RADAR

Everyone wants an easy life. People would much rather work smart than work hard. It's human nature to find the simplest way through a problem. Part of your soft-skills approach, then, is to make life easy for people. Let's say there's someone out there who needs just the service that you provide. Do they scrabble around trying to find that business card you gave them

18 months ago at a dinner party? Or have you kept yourself on their radar so that they know exactly how to reach you?

Remind people that you exist by contacting all your current and potential clients for a brief chat. If you can't get them on the phone, email has now, of course, become an equally good chatting and networking tool. Exchange useful bits of information or business gossip, and take the opportunity to reinforce your likeability, making them feel comfortable with you (see page 20). Keeping the contact short, relaxed and filled with interest automatically puts you back on their radar.

Within a month or so, I bet you'll notice that new business starts rolling in from the very people you just contacted. Your services and contact details were fresh in their mind, and, if you emailed, were also still in their inbox.

As you know, the emails that you send, although still existing within your target's inbox, quickly disappear from the display screen. They have, in effect, "dropped off". If we cannot see them, we tend to forget about them and not bother scrolling down. This is one reason why you need to continue putting yourself on the radar on a regular basis.

SOMEONE ELSE YOU SHOULD BE NICE TO…

Your target's assistant, PA or secretary; they are your target's gatekeeper. When you call to speak to their boss and they ask, *"What's it concerning?"* you may feel like saying, *"Never you mind, you wouldn't understand anyway … just put HIM ON!"*

But you won't. Whether calling to keep on the target's radar or through the course of an ongoing project, you must treat this assistant as you would the target person. Take your time with him/her. Ask his/her name, glean any personal information from their general conversation about lunch breaks, weekends etc., and make a note of it.

Every time you call, your charm and interest turn these people into your friends. They can put you on top of the pile or get you to the front of the queue – show that you respect them and their work, and they will look after you. Conversely, patronize or annoy them, and they can really make your life difficult. I am always amazed at the number of people who simply bark the name of the boss when an assistant answers the phone. You, on the other hand, must offer the differentiator of civility and friendliness, and it will make a world of difference.

CPS – Confidence, Positivity, Suggestion

Combining confidence, positivity and suggestion will transform the effect you have on others and enable you to exert whole new levels of influence over your colleagues, clients and partners.

CONFIDENCE

In the business world, confidence is what wins you trust, jobs, more money and a stronger network. Confidence conveys to others the impression that you are in control, that you are comfortable with a situation others may fear and that in the face of adversity you believe you will prevail. Your belief in yourself and your abilities – or the lack of it – is easily picked up on by people around you. Your confidence will encourage people to want to be associated with you. Even if, on the inside, you are shaking like a dog at the vet.

What do I mean by this? By definition, surely, a confident person is not quaking in their boots in such situations? In reality, however, confidence can be simulated – you can fake it. This, incidentally, is at the core of CBT (cognitive behavioural therapy), in which the basic idea is that if you change a particular outward behaviour, you will gradually change on the inside. In other words, the more you pretend to be confident, the more you will gradually become so – it will become second nature.

With this in mind, however, you should never express your fears and doubts to your targets or potential clients – save it for close confidants and family, unassociated with the pitch in hand. Obviously, if you approach a potential client with the words *"Now you are probably going to hate this idea but …"* it's over before it has even begun.

Simply introducing the word "hate" will encourage people to think negative thoughts before they even hear your idea. When I coach my political and corporate leaders to deal with the media, I advise never repeating the word that is thrown at them. If you repeat the "accusatory" word, you give it credibility – so be wary of the words you use to flag or describe what it is you are about to say.

If you wander up to a great-looking guy in a bar and say, *"Hi, my name is Lisa, I really hope you are going to like me, 'coz most guys seem to be repelled by me and I bet you already think I'm awful ..."* you're, clearly, not likely to get a date. If you are not confident in yourself or your idea, why on earth should anyone else be?

Far more effective is an approach where you exude a calm confidence (not an unpleasant arrogance) where your words, image and body language convey that this person is lucky to be meeting you and hearing your ideas. They need you; not the other way around. You are bringing something to the table, something that this person will truly appreciate.

EXAMPLE

"A lot of my clients have really gone for this approach, and it is my opinion that it could help make your sales drive even more successful ..." OK, I'm interested. I may eventually reject the idea, but so far I am still listening and that is what counts. Your confidence in the idea is contagious and creates interest in both the idea itself and you as the person capable of delivering it.

You *are* your ideas. When you sell a concept or a new way of thinking, you are selling yourself as much as you are selling the idea. The client is asking himself, *"Can this guy deliver? Does he look like he has done this before? Do I want my people to be like him? Do I like him? Do I like being around him?"* These are all crucially important questions spinning through the mind of any prospective client or contact. These are the very same thoughts we all have when confronted with having to select a doctor, a lawyer, a mechanic or a babysitter: *"Can I trust him/her to do the job well? Do I believe he has confidence in him/herself?"*

I started to discover early on that, when I sold my coaching product to new clients, their decision was swayed as much by my attitude, confidence and "professional poise" as it was by the promised results of the coaching sessions themselves. It was almost as if these clients were thinking to themselves, *"Hey, if our people could be a bit more like this guy, that's gotta be a good thing."* I had become the walking, talking personification for my product.

Obviously, confidence alone is not enough. You can't be all talk and no action – you do also have to deliver the goods: your hard skills. As a cautionary tale, I remember a fascinating man from my stockbroking days. Let's call him Bob. He arrived as the new head of the UK desk at Merrill Lynch with much fanfare. People were talking about how talented this guy was, how his interview had been filled with ideas and how he had really shaken up the last place where he had worked. This was all impressive hype, I can tell you.

He sailed through his honeymoon period, but soon things headed south somewhat. His performance was disappointing; he was always on the phone with friends (leaning back, feet on the desk, hands behind head), he created few new ideas and generated no income. Within three months, he was paid off handsomely (to leave!) and immediately landed another stunning job at a new investment bank.

It turned out that Bob gave spectacularly impressive interviews, but never delivered on the promise. I naturally applaud his ability to win over strangers; he obviously had excellent soft skills and was a powerful "self-seller". If he could only have delivered as well, he probably would now be heading up Goldman Sachs.

CONFIDENCE, NOT ARROGANCE

There is, of course, a very fine line between confidence and arrogance. It's all too easy for a confident stride to become an arrogant swagger. The trick is staying on the confident side of that line – just. How can you tell where that line is?

Well, the closer you get, the tougher it can be to discern. Once again, it is about putting yourself in the other person's shoes. It draws upon your ability to read other people, knowing what it is they react well to, delivering it, then pulling back.

How do you think they are perceiving you? What are they thinking about the words coming out of your mouth? How enthralled are they with you so far? If you keep going in your current vein, will that improve or worsen the situation?

Take a moment now to consider who in your world you would classify as arrogant or full of themselves. Make a little list of, say, three people. Think about their negative qualities, what is it you really dislike about them, what people say about them behind their backs. Write those things down, and try never to behave that way yourself!

That dividing line between confidence and arrogance is in different places for different people. If someone is a quiet, perhaps spiritual person, they may well become tired of your over-exuberance sooner than a hotshot sales manager who wants someone who can challenge and grow his young team. You have to read the situation on an individual basis and adjust your pitch accordingly. It may simply require an adjustment in tone of voice or body language, and these are things we will be exploring in later chapters.

CONFIDENCE IN ACTION

Imagine you are part of a group meeting around a boardroom table. Looking around you at this meeting, you suddenly realize that you are succeeding in getting your proposal accepted. Your confidence is paying off. Signs that this is happening include lots of nodding heads, reaffirmation or, better, the repetition of your words. Positive questions enhance your comments rather than negatively challenge your ideas.

You have already established yourself as this confident person, with a good proposal, and have earned some corporate respect. As the meeting progresses, knowing that you are ahead, ease back a little and let others speak and be heard. Your impact has been intense – like a fabulous wine. Let them savour it, think about it for a while and come back for more. If you continue to push, your confidence could seem aggressive or impatient, and you will provoke resistance, undoing all your good work. The fact is, precisely because you are confident, you don't need to be desperate, you don't need to push too hard.

Remember this cardinal rule:

WHEN IT'S GOING WELL, DON'T OVERSELL!

CONFIDENCE IS CONTAGIOUS

A winning smile, a relaxed and confident air, a warm and natural charm can win over almost anyone. And confidence can be very contagious. I've seen whole rooms become infected with it in the course of my work.

I was once in a meeting with the marketing director of an IT firm, helping him to plan a conference. With us were several junior members of the team, and two guys from a communications and events firm. We needed to devise a method where the audience could ask questions. The marketing director didn't want a free-for-all, but a more controlled interactive session.

The guys from the communications firm seemed a little unsure and raised doubts about the idea. They then made their biggest mistake. They revealed that they hadn't done a Q & A session "like this" before. They completely undermined themselves – their previous confidence lost all its power. After all, how could they say with confidence it would or wouldn't work if they had never done it before? This revelation alarmed the marketing director – I could see it in her face! We had reached an impasse.

I suggested a solution to the two communication guys (not the marketing director, as I didn't want to appear to be going over their heads, even though, actually, I really did want to do that). I revealed that at a conference only a month ago, we had done a Q & A session involving pre-submitted question cards, using special conference mailboxes. Then I, as host, was able to hold up the cards and ask the questions on behalf of the audience. The clients had been able to post a few questions of their own to help shape the direction of the forum. I offered to find out where they had got these mailboxes from because *"we could possibly use the same thing"*. I made a few other comments such as, *"I know this will work well,"* and *"Delegates will truly feel part of this session"*.

My confidence that this format would work, driven by my experience of the previous event, was what the client needed to hear. And because I made my suggestion to the communications guys, not the client, it didn't look as if I was trying to steal their show and they didn't feel put out. But I knew that my confidence in the idea won some valuable points.

The truth is that I wasn't entirely sure that this approach would work for this new event, as it was going to be so much bigger than the previous one. Also, I had thought that the mailboxes looked a bit rubbish. However, none of that counted. All that mattered was that, by delivering a solution with confidence, I was able to further validate my role and add to their confidence in me as a member of that team, and we were all able to move on quickly.

INVOKE PAST SUCCESSES

Another great way to instil confidence in others is to refer to what existing clients or contacts have said about you. Clearly this cannot be a crude statement of smug self-satisfaction – *"Well, everyone thinks I'm great, and so do I!"* Rather it needs to relate to specific achievements relevant to the new client to whom you are pitching. By referring to the comments of your top clients, especially if these are people whom your new target may know or respect, you create a situation where your clients are remotely selling you. These are their words, after all, not yours. This can be far more powerful than any words you could say about yourself.

> *"We are thrilled that so many clients come back to us time and time again. They tell us that we deploy our innovative solutions quicker than the competition and keep the costs down. It's our job to keep them happy …"*

Listening to this statement, a potential client is going to want you to start keeping them happy, too. If other clients are saying that you are fast and better priced, then it must be true. If you said it about yourself, it could just be an empty boast.

Clearly you can't fabricate wonderful recommendations from imaginary clients; the potential new client might call your bluff and ask to speak to one of them. If this happens, you will need to to produce this happy client!

POSITIVITY

Using the power of positivity in business or social relationships is highly effective. No one responds well to negativity. Indeed, your positive or negative attitude to life, just like your confidence or lack of it, can be infectious. Imagine the scene: you come stumbling into a meeting droning on about the appalling state of the trains, your hateful boss or the fact that this weather makes you want to kill yourself. Carry on like that and I can guarantee that soon everyone in the room will want to help you do it!

Or let's imagine you have been dating someone for a few weeks and you are still getting to know each other. Despite an immediate need for a bit of emotional reassurance for some reason, now is not the time to collapse in a puddle confessing that you have no clue where your career is going and that you think everyone hates you. Save that sort of outpouring for longer-standing confidants. The new lover in this example may have been daydreaming about a solid future with you – this sorry display could quickly shatter that illusion.

On the other hand, think back to the time when someone last paid you a compliment, or praised you for work well done, or gave you really fantastic service in a restaurant. The effect, I'm sure, was uplifting. That's the sort of effect you want to be having on people every day.

Remember, it is not always necessary to *truly* feel a certain way to in order to *appear* that way. Yes, it's harder to stay cheerful and positive when you are in a bad mood or have a headache, but even then, with a few simple actions or well-chosen words, you can have anyone believing that being around you is still generally a good thing. Your new-found approach will have people feeling good about you and, believe it or not, will actually make *you* feel brighter, too.

So, the mantra for this lesson is:

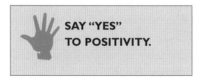

SAY "YES"
TO POSITIVITY.

POSITIVITY IN ACTION

This is all very interesting, but what does it have to do with achieving success in business you may ask? Well, take this positivity into the workplace and you instantly become someone other people want to work with. It enhances your "likeability", the importance of which we've already looked at.

Let's look at a couple of simple workplace scenarios. You're in a brainstorming session to generate new ideas for new business. Use your judgement here – after all, you don't want to become associated with the bad ideas, only the good ones! But try to react, initially at least, to flawed suggestions or daft comments with a degree of optimism. Instead of snorting in contempt and shooting it down in flames – *"That's the worst idea I have ever heard. Why do they even employ you?"* – try something like, *"Well, that's certainly interesting – I wonder if we could create something out of that."* Next, use the opportunity to show your willingness to look for better alternatives, or perhaps present an idea of your own.

Or, on entering that earlier meeting, instead of having a long moan, try at least to inject some humour or irony into the situation. Shake the rain off your umbrella, saying, *"Can't wait to get some time in the sun"* or *"Well, that journey was interesting!"* You still have the opportunity to vent a bit of your frustration, but can at least show that you can retain your sense of humour. Remember, in front of anyone who matters – the boss, a new client, a new love interest – irony and light sarcasm are good, anger and bitterness are bad!

I should add a slight caveat to my encouragement of this unrelenting optimism. It is a sweeping generalization, but the national temperament of Great Britain does tend to be a bit cooler, rather like its weather. Many Brits suffer from *schadenfreude* – delight in other people's downfall or failure. We have an entire TV soap opera dedicated to *schadenfreude* called *Eastenders*. After a half-hour episode of *Eastenders,* the general reaction is to conclude that your life really isn't *that* bad after all. Many Brits use the misery of others to make themselves feel better. So, when in London, Manchester, Birmingham, Liverpool or wherever, you may want to curb your enthusiasm for life just a touch!

SUGGESTION

The power of suggestion is one of the wonders of soft skills – it is a soft way to sell, usually far more effective than the hard sell. It is all about anticipation and desire. When you suggest an outcome to someone that is too attractive to resist – and thus land that great new contract or arrange a date with that gorgeous person you've just met – you are making the power of suggestion work for you.

Suggestion is not about getting someone to do what *you* want; rather it entails figuring out what it is the other person needs or desires, and helping them to visualize that you are the one who can give it to them. Let *them* make the decision that it is you whom they need. You merely suggest the outcome – tease them with the potential.

A beautiful woman will often be told that she is beautiful. That is now a given for her – so what does she really want to hear? Maybe she wants to hear that you find her smart, funny or compelling. Suggest to her through your conversation that you realize that beauty is more than skin deep. Through your suggestion, you will have differentiated yourself. She will be intrigued to find out more about someone who wants to get to know her properly.

Big companies are continually being told that they should partner with this firm or that one. What does the key executive really want to hear? Enough with the partnering and the deals. What they want is a differentiator – something that shows that you fully understand their needs and can solve their challenges. Your research indicates that it is a "clear, easily deployed solution where costs are minimized". All you have to do now is include this "solution" as a suggestion within your conversation. Your suggestion, which matches their actual business objective, is a hugely powerful "sell".

SUGGESTION IN ACTION

I use the power of suggestion all the time in my work. I recently met a very senior executive at a powerful software firm. He had just been promoted and was feeling the pressure when it came to making presentations at board level. The problem was that over recent months he had endured a number of poorly selected and badly performing "presentation" coaches, reducing his faith in the whole concept.

After spending a few minutes with him, I could see that he was impatient and had pretty much given up on the idea. So, instead of directly selling what I would do for him – after all, this is what those previous coaches had done, but failed to deliver on – I suggested to him an outcome that he would relish by revealing it as part of *another* client's success story.

Given his need to take his game higher – to a more senior and credible position – I decided that the key word here had to be "presidential". So, in among general chat, I revealed how a client of mine in the United States had recently had disappointing results with the media; nor was he being taken very seriously by his colleagues. I knew that this British client in front of me also had many buddies and social relationships within his organization and, as a result, had so far failed to acquire the *gravitas* that befitted his new senior position.

I continued:

> *"What I did with him, was to alter 'our' approach. We shifted content and delivery to make him more … 'presidential'. The media and his colleagues really started to listen."*

My use of the word "our" here suggested the teamwork between me, the coach, and him, the client: another message reinforcing the idea that we could work together. By this point I had generated sufficient interest from this client that he really wanted to try it, too.

By suggesting that I had helped one of my other clients to become exactly what this guy wanted to be, I rose above the other coaches out there. I had found my differentiator and gained a new client, all by the power of suggestion.

The Use of Language

GOOD WORDS, BAD WORDS

In his book about understanding first impressions, *Blink*, Malcolm Gladwell describes how the use of certain words within your conversation affects how other people feel. In any business discussion, there are two basic ways to communicate your ideas and thinking.

The first is by presenting the *harsh truth*. Here are some examples:

> *"We'll do our best to overcome any problems you will have."*
> *"This deal may become protracted and, even though we are optimistic, no doubt there'll be some bumps on the way."*
> *"I'm sure things will work out, but I'm not sure how long it will take."*

Key words here that imply a whole world of negativity are: "problems", "protracted", "bumps" and "not sure". The same thoughts, however, could be conveyed in an altogether more optimistic fashion – the *positive truth*.

> *"We look forward to guiding you safely through the challenges ahead."*
> *"We will get you through this deal as quickly and as successfully as possible."*
> *"Things are certainly looking good, and we are well on the way to a done deal."*

Here the positive words are: "safely", "quickly", "successfully", "good" and "deal". You are not misleading or telling lies, you are simply delivering the message from another perspective and direction – one that leaves people feeling better about their interaction with you. Tiny changes such as this tilt the scales in your favour.

Even when discussing unfavourable facts, figures and scenarios, it is always important to use upbeat vocabulary. This is not to advocate a perversion of the truth. But you can put a subtle spin on things to reflect well on you – that you are still in control, can find solutions to problems and remain committed to overcoming any obstacles.

BAD NEWS, GOOD NEWS

Rarely in business does any project or contract run entirely to plan. One inevitably encounters unforeseen problems, delays and extra expenses. Thus in business conversation we frequently have to reveal two sides to a situation, the good and the bad. The crucial question is: are you going to be the bearer of just bad news, or some good news as well? Are you just going to come to your client with a problem? Or can you offer them a range of solutions? At the end of the meeting, are they going to feel worried and disappointed, or still confident in your ability to make things work out right? First impressions are crucial, but last impressions count, too.

To illustrate this point, I want to tell you about a TV feature I filmed for *GMTV* – a breakfast TV broadcaster in the United Kingdom. We were putting together a story on how to open a restaurant. It was a basic "fluff" piece that skimmed the surface of what can be a huge project. We interviewed the chef-owner of this new place in Hampstead, northwest London. I asked him what his most important purchase had been. I was thinking ovens, furniture, maybe the crockery or the art on the walls. His answer surprised me. He felt that the most crucial acquisition had, in fact, been the coffee machine.

I asked him to elaborate. He explained that the last taste people had in their mouths when they left his restaurant was the coffee. He firmly believed that, if he used a cheap machine and ruined this last moment, his customers would remember only that bitter aftertaste. Humans do have selective memories, and so it made excellent sense to me that this fine chef was deliberately trying to make the final moments people spent in his restaurant as enjoyable and memorable as possible.

Now let's apply this principle to a business situation. Let's say your building project has been dogged by local-government red tape. The value of the land has gone up, but unfortunately so have the costs. How you reveal these pieces of news is very important. In order to leave a favourable last impression, you need to reveal the bad news first, then counter it with the good.

How the *bad* feels:

"About your building, yeah, well, the market value has risen, but the local government people are making life really difficult and, on top of that, the costs have gone through the roof."

Result: your client will lose the initial good news in the pessimism of the bad; if he's already having a bad day, he may be considering jumping off the very building that you are constructing – onto a government bureaucrat with any luck. As for his confidence in you, his contractors, it will most definitely be on the wane. Another piece of bad news and he could consider sacking you.

Now let's look at how the *good* news feels – the same information, but presented the right way:

"About your building, yeah, OK, we are trying to manage these awkward local government people, and looking at ways to reduce the increased costs, but the good news is that the value of the entire property has risen faster than we thought. This will easily offset the extra expenditure, so overall this is looking great!"

Result: Hooray, this is good news. Not sure what you were saying about those government guys, but it sounds as if you've got it under control. As for the increased value bit, fantastic, I'm gonna be rich! Love you guys. Keep it up!

CONCLUSION

We've explored a huge range of core soft skills in this chapter. A lot of it has to do with appearances, cultivating friendship, developing your likeability, and so on. People have said to me in the past, *"It's all about being fake, isn't it?"* I completely understand this viewpoint and, to an extent, there is some truth there. But, when you think about it, we are all faking it every day of our lives. After all, do we always tell people exactly what we think of them? Do we never bite our tongues to stay out of trouble? When there is someone at work who you really can't stand, do you tell them or do you attempt to fake niceties to keep everyone calm and even-keeled?

We regularly disguise our true feelings, maintain a professional front and get the job done.

However, I like to be a bit more upfront and explicit about the strategic communication and soft skills we can all use in order to make our business as successful and fulfilling as possible. That way you can retain more control over what people think of you and the decisions they actually make.

There are still plenty more soft-skills ideas to add to your arsenal. Before you can employ them, however, we need to look at your image – the very first impression you make.

CHAPTER 2

Your Image, Your Brand

> Think of successful people you know – personally, and
> through the media. How do they come across? Is there
> such a thing as a successful image, a wealthy look?
> Those who think there is will cite clothes, cars,
> jewellery and other accessories, along with perhaps a
> suntan or a certain "worldliness". Those who think it's
> a myth – after all there are plenty of exceptions to the
> rule – will still observe the value of confident
> presentation, deportment, an intelligent expression
> and a healthy appearance.

NO DIVING – SHALLOW END

What do I mean by that heading? Simply that we are now in
at the shallow end of the soft-skills tool pool! Of course, it
would be great if we lived in a world where every single person was
perceptive and profound enough for body image and fashion not to matter.
But the fact is, they *do* matter and, until that utopian world arrives, you'd
better start working the existing system to your maximum advantage.

Whether we like to admit it or not there is a part of all of us – and that
includes our target clients – that judges on appearances. We are all making
split-second judgements about people every day. Just by walking past
someone in the street we probably think we have an idea of their income
bracket, their family background, even their state of mind. So in the world
of business, this is something of which you must take advantage.

I hope by now that you agree that we are *all* in sales. If not, please return
to the Introduction! Part of the success – or failure – of that sales pitch is your
image. You obviously want to project an image of confidence and success.

WHY DOES IMAGE MATTER?

Just in case you're not still entirely convinced, here are some
reminders about why image is so important:

1 You are constantly being judged

People are constantly weighing you up. They are checking you out,
examining you up and down. Even though little is said, you are being
scored on an ongoing basis. You lose points for scruffy shoes and gain
points for a Breitling watch; lose points for chipped nail varnish and
gain points for coordinated accessories.

2 Image counts

Despite all best intentions not to be superficial, image *does* matter,
and every time you add to that image in a positive way you win more
points. I'm not saying that this is a good thing, but it *is* a real thing.
This is the way the world works, and we're not in the business here
of changing that, but rather of making it work for you. The fact is that
you can't beat them – so dress up and start winning.

3 You are in charge

With your daily clothing and presentation choices, you are telling the
world who you are, what you stand for and what you want. No one
else makes this choice for you. With your choice of look, you are
telling people who they are really dealing with – you are helping to
influence the way that you are perceived.

4 Expect the unexpected

How can you be sure that on the day you wear your oldest suit or
fail to change those laddered pantyhose that the most important
person in your life isn't about to walk in? Always dress to impress.

The simple truth is that we like to be around good-looking people and things. Who can deny that they are attracted to beautiful art, sleek shiny cars, white sandy beaches, unspoiled countryside, sexy models – not necessarily in that order! Conversely, we steer clear of rotting trash piles, smelly subway platforms, bad attitudes and repugnant people.

Decades of studies and statistical data have shown that people who are better presented, better looking and more attractive do a whole lot better in life. Shocking as it may seem, according to Allan and Barbara Pease in their book *Why Men Lie and Women Cry*, it has been shown that in the United States "attractive men are paid 12–14% more" than their ordinary-looking colleagues. In addition, a study in Pennsylvania discovered that better-looking "suspects" received lighter sentences and often no jail time at all, compared to unattractive defendants accused of the same crimes.

By the way, if you really want to know how attractive the rest of the world thinks you are, you may wish to submit your photo to a website – www.hotornot.com – where online surfers get to look at your picture, judge how cute (or not) you may be and then award you a score out of 10. Painful, but at least honest!

Of course, there are certain things we cannot change about our appearance. Despite hours in the gym or even plastic surgery, we cannot all look like Brad Pitt or Scarlett Johansson. But what we can do is make the absolute best of what we have.

Remember my advice about those tiny differentiators (see Introduction, pages 15–16)? Well, your image and presentation are crucial contributions to your differentiator score. Make that extra effort and it could make the difference between you being someone people remember and say *"Yes"* to, or not even registering on their radar – being someone who ultimately ends up on the reject pile.

Your image is indeed about how you *look*, but it is also about how you *appear*. Thus, even if you're not blessed with matinée-idol looks, an air of confidence can be more than ample compensation. Good presentation can feed this confidence. Step out of the door immaculately groomed and dressed in your best suit, and you will instantly hold your head higher and feel ready to face anything.

Personal Grooming

Let's start at the very beginning. Personal grooming largely involves mere details, some of which your target may not even notice. But overall the package will be noticed. After all, if you cannot take care of yourself, how on earth are you going to take care of your client? Just as importantly, good grooming will make you feel that you are presenting yourself at your best. How you feel and the perception that creates in others are paramount.

While women have for millennia realized the advantages of using cosmetics and toiletries, men have quickly cottoned on in recent decades, as the sales figures testify. So you have no excuse not to moisturize and look after your skin during the dry winter months, just as much as the ladies!

MIRROR MIRROR

Obvious stuff but, if you've just stepped off a plane or out of a hot and sticky subway, it can be difficult to walk into that important meeting looking shower-fresh. Always make sure you build enough time into your travel arrangements to pay a visit to the bathroom to freshen up.

Clothes

Your clothing choice is one of the most visible and obvious demonstrations of who you really are. *"Oh sure, I have suits and outfits that are five years old, but they're still OK aren't they?"* No, I'm afraid they are not!

It is no longer acceptable to throw on any old thing because you have no major meetings that day or to neglect your hair or makeup because you don't have a hot date. From here on I want you to consider such acts as "clothing crimes" – I'm the clothing police ensuring that you never breach that law again!

WHO HAVE YOU COME AS?

When thinking about the impression you want to make, it might help to think of someone you wish to emulate – a form of positive thinking that gives you a subtle direction to consider. Whose public image do you most respect or admire? Whether it's Jennifer Garner, Brad Pitt, Helen Mirren or George Clooney, when refreshing your image, having a goal in mind can really help you to focus on what works for you. Do they have certain trademark looks or wear certain designers whose clothes always tend to look good on them? Would that look suit you?

Experiment a bit and, before you know it, you'll have found a look that's uniquely yours (even if it is slightly "borrowed" from someone you admire). You must dress to suit yourself – not as a poor imitation of someone else. As much as some of us try to hide or disguise our age, the best impression you will make is with an outfit that looks about right for your years and that is classically stylish as opposed to immediately fashionable.

DESIGNER LABELS

Labels are something to aspire to and use sparingly. With a limited budget it's all too easy to decide to have no designer presence at all in the wardrobe. But in the same way that people will "ooh" and "aah" about a fabulous new car, they'll do the same for a sharp Gucci suit or a stylish Varvatos sweater. You don't have to go completely "label" but having a little bit in most outfits works great and continues to put you ahead of the rest.

If you are going to spend money like this, you want to invest in looks that have some staying power. If you feel that you must ditch an entire outfit after a single season, you didn't choose as well as you could have done. Select high-quality looks that ooze style and the investment will stay with you for two to three years, not two to three months.

ACCESSORIES

If you're working within a budget, accessories could be the area in which you splash out on something really top quality. A perfectly average outfit can look so much sharper and more impressive if accompanied by a superb tie or killer designer handbag. And, if you have invested in a $2,000 suit, don't let it down by wearing a plastic belt, will you? Again, ladies tend to be ahead of the guys in the accessories stakes. They've been doing it for centuries, and certainly don't need my advice! Gents, on the other hand, are only just beginning to pay attention to these things. So here follows some advice to help us to catch up.

GENTLEMEN – THIS BIT IS JUST FOR YOU

I trust you are on top of this already, but I feel obliged to guide you in one very important style direction. Shoes! It is astounding how often a great outfit and look can be ruined by a scruffy pair of shoes.

I fully appreciate that we blokes like our value. If you've spent $300 on a pair of shoes, you fully expect them to last 10 years … and even if they don't you are still going to wear them for that decade regardless! Tragically, this is not a good idea. A good pair of shoes will last you two to three years; then, for reasons of fashion and wear-and-tear, they need to be replaced.

If you dress in a suit, people will *always* judge you on your shoes, so this is one area where you should certainly not skimp and save. You should be spending between $400 and $600 (£200 and £300) on your main business shoes. Depending on your outfit colour choices, you may well need two pairs. Breaking this cost down, across three years, you are looking at a monthly expenditure (for one pair at $600) of $16. Go without one bottle of wine every month and you have your fabulous-looking shoes.

Need ideas? Consult with fashionably aware friends, most women or magazines such as *Arena* and *GQ*. Decide on a look that suits your individuality, then, armed with timely, accurate price information, you can make your choice.

I know what you're thinking: shoes can't really be that important, can they? Surely I'm obsessed with an item of clothing that you know you can pick up far more cheaply … and you'd be right.

Yes, you can go to Marks & Spencers in London or Macy's in New York and pick up the cheap option, and probably get away with it just fine. In a world where you are trying to maximize every little differentiator in your favour, however, here is a chance to improve your score. By investing

in top-end shoes, you show that you recognize quality when you see it and appreciate the finer things in life. This will all reflect on your business judgement and acumen. Look after your shoes as the investment they are, and watch how things start happening for you!

Also, outside the business world, if you happen to be single and looking for a good woman, you should note that women absolutely adore a smart pair of shoes on a man – they may even refer to them when describing a date to their friends!

If people are going to notice your shoes, they are also going to notice what you put in them. Don't waste the shoes investment by pairing them with Bart Simpson socks – it just makes you look like a child who has not yet matured sufficiently to dress like a man. Just as importantly, make sure you are wearing matching socks!

WHAT TIME IS IT?

A smart watch shows a sense of personal care and style. Invest wisely in something that isn't a GPS digital bonanza. Some stylists and commentators claim that men should not buy a watch that is too thin or delicate-looking. As a man, they claim, you want to appear strong and in control, and so you should proudly be wearing a heavy-looking chunky silver (not gold – too bling!) watch. Tag, Breitlinger, Omega may well be inspirational brands.

SIZE LIES

Your choice of clothing must be comfortable enough for you to perform your daily tasks and yet tailored enough to show off any contours worth showing off. You would think that choosing the right size of clothing would be a pretty basic task, but there are many people who still get this spectacularly wrong. The most common cause of this is when you have gained weight but not upgraded your wardrobe accordingly. Some people insist on buying clothes in the size they fitted into 10 years ago, in a subconscious refusal to admit that their body shape may have changed.

Male or female, I cannot stress what a terrible mistake this is. There is nothing worse than seeing shirt buttons straining and exposing pockets of flesh, or "Muffin Top" – rolls of tummy bulging over the top of waistbands. In extreme cases it can be utterly distracting, and could completely undermine the brilliant sales pitch you may be giving. Colleagues and potential clients will notice this lack of judgement, then start to talk about it – it could become something you are known for, rather than your business prowess, technical expertise or sales abilities.

Rather than squeezing into clothes two sizes too small, invest in smart, comfortable tailored clothes that fit you properly. If you are concerned about your weight, well-fitting clothes will actually make you look far slimmer than those that are too small. If you do shed the pounds in the future, then great – you can go and reward yourself with a new wardrobe! But in the meantime you will still have been looking great and not have undermined your professional image.

LUCKY CLOTHES

We may not admit it, but, proudly positioned in all our wardrobes and closets, each of us probably has one or two items of "lucky" clothing. These could be anything from lucky shoes or lucky shirts, to lucky ties, lucky pants or lucky bras!

You will know if you have one of these key pieces of clothing because you will deliberately save it up for special occasions, meetings and events. The psychology behind this lucky item of clothing is simple. One day in the past you will have achieved something great, maybe a pay rise or a new job or a fabulous contract with a brand new client. You will have returned home that evening, looked at yourself in the mirror, smiling with pride, and instead of praising your brilliant actions will have associated that day's success with the outfit you were wearing. You'll say to yourself, *"It can't have been me; it must have been these trousers!"* And they become your "lucky trousers", destined to be worn on every special occasion and at every crucial meeting.

What really happened, of course, was that you looked good. Without you fully realizing it, the clothing that you selected on that successful day made you feel confident, successful and strong. The clothes looked good on you, and as a result you exuded confidence. When you display confidence, people want to be associated with you.

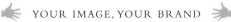

The moral of this story is that you must ensure that *all* your clothes make you look fantastic. In fact, to go one step further, I would advise that, from now on, you should spend a lot of money on clothes – at least, far more than you are accustomed to. This may be a tough one to sell at home, but, trust me, the items you buy will be an investment in your success and your future. You owe it to yourself to *know* that you look good. The air of confidence, literally streaming off you, will serve you very well indeed.

THE DOS AND DON'TS OF CLOTHING

- DO look stylish and up to date, but not ultra fashionable.

- DO be aware of the "stop wearing by" date for any item – work on a two-season maximum.

- DO wear clothes that fit just right and accentuate your assets.

- DO dress for your (realistic) target image.

- DO care for your clothing.

- DON'T try to be too sexy for work or too conservative for play.

- DON'T neglect your personal grooming.

- DO make sure you occasionally get noticed and appreciated for your clothing choice.

- AVOID bad or rushed decisions by planning an outfit the night before.

Our Bodies

Strip off and look in the mirror… go on. Well? Awful? Adequate? Fabulous? Most of us are dissatisfied with the way we look – don't worry; it's normal. Even people who look fabulous will have something about their bodies they hate. If you are one of the few people who look in the mirror and exclaim *"Wow, check me out. Ooh, yeah, I am hot!"* **please skip this section and report immediately to the nearest modelling agency.**

The good news for the rest of us is that with enough motivation you can, of course, change the way you look – whether it's losing weight or toning up – through a sensible and balanced diet, enough regular exercise and a realistic target.

LOSE WEIGHT, GAIN CONFIDENCE

Most people who lose weight will share a similar story. They will all cite one day, one comment, that motivated them sufficiently to start a diet. For me it was seeing myself live on a television monitor in the TV studio where I was working and having a co-presenter tell me that I looked a little… porky. Not nice but, unfortunately for me, quite accurate!

When that moment comes for any of us, we have choices. We either do something about it or ignore it and decide that it simply does not matter. In my case I had to do something about it because, in my industry with the people who choose to work in it, looking less than great was not an option. If I didn't lose major weight, my television career wouldn't be taking me anywhere.

So, propelled by those stinging remarks and my own harsh observations, I embarked on a period of eating less (which was very difficult because I absolutely love my food) and exercising a lot more (which was not difficult as I hadn't exercised at all up until that point). After six months I was 35 pounds lighter, and my confidence was at an all-time high.

Although the weight coming off was a great result in its own right, what I hadn't fully anticipated was how much my business would change as a result. Suddenly, new offers started coming in – fresh speaking engagements and more coaching work. It became clear to me that people were associating my achievement of weight loss with success, willpower and motivation.

For anyone who does not work in TV or the public eye, body image may not be quite so important. But if you are carrying some extra pounds, the biggest favour you can do for your confidence, not to mention your health, is to find the motivation and incentive to do something about it.

HEALTHY TO WEALTHY

People react to a slimmer/fitter/more tanned you in ways that will truly be a surprise. Suddenly there are new opportunities, new invites, fresh offers. More people will want to know you. People who do not fit the above descriptions still, of course, meet with huge success. However, I would argue that their brilliance and confidence simply outshine any physical imperfections. Conversely, I doubt many people have ever become a great success story by dressing like a slob and gaining 100 pounds!

The suntan has long been the hallmark of the rich and famous. It conveys that you are such a success in your profession that you can afford to jet off to tropical climes to maintain that year-round tan. Now, of course, we are all aware of the dangers of skin cancer and accelerated ageing that too much exposure to the sun's rays can cause. Nevertheless, the association of a tan with wealth and success remains as strong as ever in many people's minds – people are still attracted to this appearance.

So there's no reason why we can't add a glow to our skins to look a little healthier and encourage confidence in who we are. Rather than the potentially harmful sun-bed option, try out some of the advanced fake tanning creams and gels that proliferate in our department stores. If it's your first time, try a little on a Saturday morning and see how it works on your skin. You just want a healthy glow, not to look bright orange!

WHAT'S FOR LUNCH? A FACELIFT?

Don't laugh or scoff, but, there's always the option of a little cosmetic surgery. (I told you we were in at the shallow end!) It's a very serious and personal decision, and not something I would dream of advising on either way. But I want to draw attention to the effect it can have on you as a person after the work has been completed and you have sufficiently healed.

If you are the type of person who would love to have a little Restylane or Botox or a facial peel or other such treatment, you should do it. If you are thrilled with the results, just as with lucky clothes or losing weight, your whole demeanour will change. Your new levels of confidence will, once again, be tangible. People will want to be associated with the positive vibes coming off you and you will meet with higher levels of success due directly to how you feel about yourself.

WALK TALL NOT SMALL

Shirley Bassey said it best, many years ago. The minute you walk into a room, you want people to regard you as a person of distinction. In any situation, whether networking, at a party or in a meeting, the way that you enter a room and people's line of sight says a lot about the person you are.

Many of us are natural-born slouchers and we fail to make an impact in any room entry. But good posture and confident body language can immediately catch the eye and mark you out as someone other people will be interested in meeting.

From frogs to apes to bears in critical situations, most animals make themselves look as big and powerful as possible. In the rest of the animal kingdom, it's a case of puffing out your feathers, fur, face or plumage in order to attract a mate or become leader of the pack. In our world, it's somewhat more subtle, but the same principle applies.

When you feel down or depressed, your entire body and facial expression may well take on a defeated, forlorn appearance. This usually manifests itself as a slouchy, bent back accompanied by the sad face and downward looking eyes. In the same way that we associate confidence with success, we also associate a lack of confidence with potential failure. So even when you're feeling down, ensure that your posture and body language are telling a totally different story.

Stand up straight, pull your tummy in, stick your chest out and attempt to look as tall as you can. Without looking like a total nutter, try to adopt and display a slight smile – the appearance of someone who is happy, certain and secure. These actions make a tiny difference, but sometimes that's all you need to swing things back into your favour again.

PICTURE PERFECT

The fabulous proliferation of cameras, whether on phones, laptops, Blackberries, PDAs or ... er ... actual cameras means that throughout your life you will be photographed a lot. Given that many of these images end up on-line – making you "Google-able" seemingly for ever, it pays to ensure that your moment in the lens makes you look as good as possible.

There are several things you can do to ensure that you maximize your positive appearance and minimize any potential embarrassment that may follow from these photo opportunities. I don't want to make you paranoid – but it pays to be properly prepared for those photo moments ... you'll thank me!

FIND SHADE

If you are out and about, and you have *any* location control, try not to stand in direct sunlight. Those hot and bright beams of light will have you squinting as if you were in a sandstorm. Position yourself in the shade of buildings or the "top shade" of trees, canopies and awnings. This allows light to gently bounce onto your face with no nasty shadows or burning brightness.

WIPE YOUR FOREHEAD

Leaf through the pages of any celebrity magazine and you will see many faces literally shining at the camera. The flash is a fearsome device the blinding light of which gets immediately reflected back into the lens. Any amount of moisture or grease on your skin will increase this effect until your head looks like an exploding supernova. Best way to deal with this is to step slightly back and make sure that you have plenty of matt anti-shine makeup on (mostly the girls), or a handkerchief or tissue to dab yourself dry, or take the time to go rinse your forehead with cold water just before your paparazzi moment. It works a treat.

STAND TO THE LEFT

Those of you who follow politics may remember a US Republican presidential candidates debate in May 2007. A huge stage was filled with a semicircle of very presidential podiums. Each candidate could stand at any podium and make his comments from there. It turned out, however, that not all podiums were equal. There was a most undignified scramble for the podium to the far left. In the event, it was Mitt Romney who made it to that pole position (even though politically he was much further to the right!).

Why this mad rush? When the photograph of all the candidates appeared in the papers the next day, it would be captioned, as all photographs are, with the words: *"Pictured, from left: Mitt Romney …"* By standing to the left, this particular politician knew that his name would be listed before all those colleagues around him.

Given the short attention span of most humans, especially when reading political stories, the chances are they won't read through to the end of the caption. Romney ensured that his name at least would get some attention. Tiny, cynical differentiator – but nice move!

SUBTLE SMILE

Big broad smiles can look a little "horsey" and sometimes a little manic – so try to perfect a smaller, knowing smile, without looking as if you are smirking. Your objective is to create a calm, confident and relaxed look. You may need to practise in the mirror – just ensure that no one is around when you do this!

SILENCE PLEASE

Most of the time, the ability to talk and entertain those around you is an important skill worth pursuing. When there is a camera pointed at you, however, you need to stem the flow of words. When that shutter opens for a fifteenth of a second, in the middle of one of your words, you can look really quite mad. For example, if you are saying, *"C'mon everyone, he's trying to take a picture …"* and the camera flashes at the "-ture" bit of your word "picture", you end up looking like a chimpanzee. Go on, try it – you'll see!

NO MUG SHOTS

If it's just you who is the subject of the photograph and you find yourself looking straight into the lens – try to adjust your position. You want to avoid a direct, straight-on stare. Instead, try to angle your head slightly away from the lens, left or right, but ensure that your eyes are making contact with the camera. This is far more flattering. Paris Hilton, she of the well-known, overly photographed, definition of fame, even found time to strike this pose in front of the police photographer when she was arrested for drink-driving. What a professional …!

No matter how good you think your image is already, I'm sure there is something extra you can be doing to make the most of your appearance. Whether it's losing 10 pounds, investing in that killer suit, having a little Botox, or getting a tan – stride like a movie star and you will feel 1,000 miles ahead of where you currently are. From the first day you follow this new approach you will feel better about yourself, and people around you will see it. A great image is a way of creating your confidence, power and even wealth.

So, now that you are looking and feeling better, and you are starting to make the most of all aspects of your image, what happens next? You have something to say! This is the focus of the next chapter.

CHAPTER 3

Voice –
Tone, Melody and Control

It occurs to me on a regular basis that many of us don't know ourselves very well – we do not have sufficient self-awareness to understand the impact we have on the people around us. We can sometimes have blind spots with regard to our faults and bizarrely believe that we may, in fact, be close to perfect.

The more senior or apparently successful someone becomes, the more this self-belief applies. Now, there is nothing wrong with a healthy dose of self-confidence, but occasionally, like a finely tuned piece of machinery, you need to conduct a self-diagnostic, an honest "self-audit".

I want you to be the best you can be. With this in mind, I would like to draw attention to one of the items that people often entirely overlook when evaluating their performance – their voice. Your voice has many components: volume, projection, diction, pace and tone.

Your voice is your single most important instrument in conveying your message. If your words are great, but your delivery of them is poor or, worse, annoying in some way, people won't want to listen to you for very long.

VOLUME

Think of the last time you were in a restaurant or on a plane or anywhere else that people may gather in a confined space. I'll wager that you could hear one or two voices above everyone else's.

I was recently dining with a client, Andrea, at a smart place in Chicago, and at the table next to us were three business sorts having a dinner meeting. Fine. Nothing wrong with that. Except that I could clearly hear one of them over the others. I heard about the value of the property deal they were working on ($20 million); I heard who he did and did not trust. I know that during the following weekend he fully intended to fly to Miami. Meanwhile, I could not hear a single word from the other two participants in the conversation – I could hear only the "shout lout"!

Setting aside the rules on dining etiquette for just a moment, this entire "broadcast" could well have been a major breach in client confidentiality… I could have been a journalist or, worse, a competitor. Walls have ears, and so do we.

But here's the thing. He clearly had no idea about his bullhorn megaphone voice. His colleagues were clearly too embarrassed or did not feel sufficiently empowered to draw attention to the fact that he was bellowing like an overexcited soccer coach; he carried on with his public pronouncements throughout dinner.

I glanced over several times and pointedly made eye contact, attempting to communicate that I could hear every word he was saying. But he was too busy enjoying listening to the sound of his own voice to bother with reading the reactions of people around him.

So, for his benefit and for the benefit of others like him, here are my three top tips regarding volume control. If any of these apply to you, you may want to turn down the volume a little:

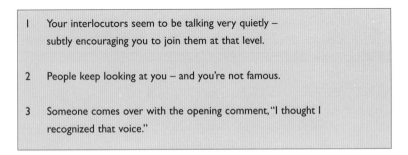

1	Your interlocutors seem to be talking very quietly – subtly encouraging you to join them at that level.
2	People keep looking at you – and you're not famous.
3	Someone comes over with the opening comment, "I thought I recognized that voice."

PACE AND DICTION

The moral of the "shout lout" tale is that you need to be aware of your environment, and modify your voice accordingly. The "shout lout" is probably great when addressing a large meeting of shareholders, but was awful in the more intimate restaurant setting.

At the other end of the spectrum, of course, is the whisperer or mumbler. Here is someone who believes that just because they can hear themselves, everyone else can hear them, too – a bit like an ostrich which, having hidden its head in the sand, believes that no part of its enormous body is now visible.

How can you tell if you are a whisperer or mumbler? If people have to lean closer and closer when you speak or consistently ask you to repeat yourself, you may need to project a little more. Mumblers often speak quietly, but also too quickly, swallowing their words and speaking as fast as they think. So, even if you have a lot to say, remember, slow down sufficiently that people can understand what you're saying.

Don't forget, the whole thrust of soft skills or strategic communication is how we affect and influence other people. We have to make everything around us feel good, right down to the volume, pitch and sound of our voices.

MELODY

When you watch TV, especially the news and breakfast TV shows, you will notice that the hosts and presenters have a certain way of speaking. Their voices are mellifluous – their words tend to flow in a pattern that sounds attractive to our ears. Their comments are filled with phrases such as *"Still to come" "Don't forget"*, and *"Just ahead"*.

This vocal embellishment is no accident. TV presenters are chosen not only for the way they look, but also for the way they sound. A good voice is never monotonous, but is punctuated with pauses, punches, rises and falls, and delivers speech in a steady rhythm. This is a major asset when trying to impart crucial information, such as how busy the roads are, whether it's going to rain or which politician is ahead in the polls.

"SIT!"

Whether talking tête-à-tête with a new lover, motivating a group of 10 employees, or addressing a conference room filled with 200 delegates, the aim is always to keep the attention of your audience, have them wanting to hear more. A perfect example of the effect of "melody" – the rise and fall in your voice – can be taken from how we deal with our fabulous tail-wagging four-legged friends.

If you want to attract the attention of your dog, you don't use a dull, lifeless voice. They won't listen, and they won't respond. Instead, you need to adopt that high-pitched, excited voice that accompanies such promising offers as *"Wanna go for walkies?"*, or *"Wanna treat? Do you? DO YOU? Yes, you do!!"* The goal here is to arouse their sense of anticipation. Usually the voice goes way up in pitch towards the end of each sentence. The tone adopted makes the offer sound so tempting that your dog is skipping around, flapping his little ears, barking with excitement about your proposal.

Now I'm certainly not saying you should burst into the CEO's office and scream *"Wanna quarterly financial report? "Do you? DO YOU?"* But if you believe that you may be at risk of sounding dull from time to time, what you can always do in any meeting, conversation or interaction is *vocally animate your voice*. Let's explore in greater detail various ways in which you can do this.

BREVITY AND THE SOUND BITE

When you are media-trained to appear as a television or radio guest "expert", you are instructed to "keep it short". In fact, the ideal length of a piece of spoken content is 20 to 25 seconds. This is known as the perfect sound bite.

Why? Well, apparently, somebody has sat down and calculated the span of attention of an average "remote-control-wielding" viewer. They concluded that the viewer will stay tuned to a channel, listening to a message for about 25 seconds, before they fundamentally need something to change. Unless the image, message, person blabbing or TV show changes, boredom may set in.

So, to meet this evident need, smart players in a media-savvy world need to truncate their words and ideas to adapt to this goldfish-like attention span. Politicians do it, sharp spokespeople do it and winning leaders seem to have a talent for reducing complex ideas, initiatives and concepts to a succinct 20-second hit.

You have to be brutal with yourself. You have to examine what it is you need to communicate and chop it down with a word-cleaver★ so that the absolute bare minimum survives.

HOW TO CHOP DOWN YOUR MESSAGE

Let's take an imaginary news story and look at long rambling version alongside the attention-grabbing sound-bite version.

Not getting to the point:

> *"A small furry black-and-white cat known to locals, and occasionally some people who live further afield, as 'Alfie' has, it would appear and despite previous warnings and some degree of training, while wandering freely in a park, which was inadvisable from the start, somehow and inexplicably, taking into consideration the absolute level of chance involved, tumbled into a well."*

This "epic" has taken up way too much of our lives. There are people who can daisy-chain a never-ending group of flowery, unnecessary sub-clauses together to create the world's largest sentence, seemingly without ever getting to the actual point. Don't let this person be you. The above example is extreme – but long, drawn-out, overly ambitious sentences fill people with a sense of entrapment and dread.

Perfect sound bite:

> *"Onlookers were shocked to discover that local cat Alfie fell into a well today – this clearly highlights the dangers of allowing cats too close to wells."*

★ *There is no such thing as a 'word cleaver'.*

With minimal fuss and elaboration, this sound bite reaches the point before people have had a chance to mentally switch off. Effective communication should quickly get the message across and not merely fill the maximum time available.

(No animals were hurt in the creation of the previous example.)

In business or personal relationships, short is sweet. Be succinct, concise and to the point. If you have any story to tell, any new initiative to pitch, frame your text around the following questions: *"Who?" "What?" "When?" "Where?"* and *"Why?"* If this excludes something you still want to tell, keep it in hand to bring out when your initial pitch has aroused such interest and enthusiasm that your audience is clamouring to know more. You can then expand further or give more detailed examples.

Remember, your audience has a short attention span. Don't bog them down with rambling, convoluted sentences. Instead, inspire people with your vision and concision of thought. Free your audience with your brevity and get to the point!

RHETORICAL QUESTIONS –
CREATE INTEREST AND COMMAND ATTENTION

Can rhetorical questions work? Do they appeal to people? Might they be your way of creating additional interest? Yes, yes and… yes! Of course, you do not live your everyday life asking rhetorical questions (certainly not out loud!): *"Would I like a Martini? Yes." "Am I happy to pay these prices? No."*

But, used sparingly, within important pitches, meetings and presentations, they are an excellent way of reinvigorating your audience and ensuring that people around you believe that you are interesting.

Facts and statistics can become tiresome and dull, but a direct or leading question needs answering, a story needs ending, we need closure. Phrasing the information you want to get across in a question–and–answer format provides the opening that facilitates this closure:

"So, exactly how many people would die in a Luxembourg-based tsunami?"
"What was the single biggest cause of food poisoning last year?"
"Which is the best way to make someone fall in love with you?"

"Shriek!" I need to know! I would listen to anyone that makes me think of questions like that! Rhetorical or leading questions can be a fantastic tool to show that you have really focused on the key issues at hand.

Rhetorical questions are like joker cards – you can't use them all the time. So, save them up and deploy when necessary.

CHAPTER 4

Networking Secrets

In the previous chapters we've been developing new attitudes and skills, and revamping your image and vocal presentation. Now we've reached the exciting bit and are going to take all these new attributes out into the real world ...

NETWORKING – A MISSED OPPORTUNITY

Whether it's beer with friends at a bar or clinking glasses with CEOs at yet another champagne reception at the Four Seasons or chatting to the guy next to you on the treadmills at the gym, this is all networking. But just because you do it, doesn't mean you couldn't do it even better. Networking is something many of us feel less than comfortable doing – you may even sneer at it as superfluous – but the fact is we could all thrive on the results if we made the most of every social encounter and networking opportunity. You must ensure that your climb to the top of the social or business ladder is liberally strewn with events where networking can work in your favour.

Incidentally, wonderful as Facebook, MySpace and LinkedIn and other such websites are, they don't represent true networking. Yes, they are a good way to build connections and contacts – but until you have met someone in the flesh and delivered your whole range of soft skills in person, the chances of engaging in some profitable business are a lot slimmer.

Being a good networker can make the difference between remaining "FBI" (friendly but ineffective) and becoming a sparkling well-connected mover and shaker, someone who continually sets the agenda, always appears comfortable and is confident with and liked by people at all levels.

Don't forget, this set of skills applies equally well to any party or social gathering, not just business encounters. You won't be discussing the price of oil and your profit margin, but instead your ability to talk and maybe flirt wittily about any number of subjects with brand-new contacts may prove just as important in networking your way to your target.

One of the keys to successful networking is, of course, confidence. Now that may not be something you naturally possess in abundance, but it is something you can simulate – you may want to review chapter 1 to brush up on your confidence-building. And, of course, mastering all the soft skills set out in this book should go a long way towards reassuring you that you possess what it takes to make a success of any business encounter, and to make any social engagement an enjoyable one.

> **GOOD NETWORKING SKILLS**
> **+ WELL-COMMUNICATED CONFIDENCE**
> **= SUCCESS**

Essential Networking Skills

In addition to the skills, attitudes and first impressions already explored in the previous chapters, there are a few more specific networking skills to add to your arsenal before we look at how to put them into practice.

THE HANDSHAKE

Aha! At last, we get to the subject behind the title of this book! For most people, their handshake is something to which they've never given a moment's thought, but the fact that a recent survey revealed that 80 per cent of people have been on the receiving end of a damp, limp, wet, weak or "bone-crushing" handshake shows that a lot of people still get this wrong. Make no mistake, the handshake can make or break a wonderful introduction.

How could these people not know? Do they think their handshake is normal? Are these tragic figures labouring under the illusion that everyone else is getting it wrong and that their limp little finger squeeze/knuckle-crunching grip is the way to go? I quickly figured out the answer. No one will ever *tell* you that you've messed up your handshake. People say nothing.

"Nice to meet you Bob, but… OUCH!! what was that?! What's up with your handshake? It's awful. What's wrong with you?" It's never going to happen. Obviously, these people simply aren't aware of the problem. Rather like with bad breath or body odour, the last one to find out about these career-limiting problems is the person in question. These subjects are generally deemed too personal or sensitive to broach, and so nothing is said.

But a handshake is such a small thing, such a brief moment in time, why does it even matter? It all goes back to the differentiators that take your score above or below 50 per cent (see pages 15-16). You won't win points with a good or normal handshake, but you can most certainly lose them with a bad one. People won't bother to remark to their friend, in hushed conspiratorial tones, *"Hey, guess what, I just shook hands with that guy, over there and … it was within expectations!"* as that just isn't news. But they certainly will lean over to whisper, *"Pssst, that guy has the sweatiest handshake ever, like a piece of salmon. Gross!"*

Imagine that someone whom you are attempting to attract or impress has maybe two or three people, including yourself, who would fit the bill for a project, pay rise, contract or job. A well-executed, friendly handshake, accompanied by the right eye contact and a pleasant smile, makes a great first impression. In most business relationships the initial handshake is the foundation on which years of business are built.

People like to work with and do deals with equals. They don't want to drag an inferior along for the ride, nor do they want the daily intimidation of someone constantly trying to appear superior. So don't ruin things at the outset by delivering an incompatible image.

Here are the golden rules for a good handshake.

DURATION

Two seconds, that's it. No more. Of course, there are cultural differences; people from the Middle East will often hold your hand for up to three minutes, for example. When travelling overseas you must make sure you are well informed beforehand about any specific national greetings or social customs. But in most circumstances, the two-second handshake will be fine.

THE LONG SHAKERS

What is up with these people who hold on for dear life? You've finished your handshake, you've weakened your grip in preparation for withdrawal and they just keep on shaking, as if they've completely forgotten to let go.

These people are committing two handshake crimes. One is that they simply don't know the ideal duration of an acceptable handshake. Fair enough. Not everyone can be as smart as you and I! The second crime is somewhat more serious. These people have no idea that *you* have finished shaking hands with them. They aren't interested in you; if they were concerned about you, they would be paying attention to your reactions and would have instantly detected that you were finished. Instead, they are so caught up in their own agenda – and whatever bizarre reasons they may have for shaking so long – that they just keep going until *they* are done. What does this say about them as someone with whom to do business? They do things their own way. They don't respond well to your needs. Not a good impression.

So, in the unlikely event that you might currently be a long shaker, remember to stay aware of the people you are meeting – if they want to stop, so do you!

EARLY SHAKERS

Many, many people suffer from ESS (Early-Shaker Syndrome). This is when a person rushes in and just squeezes the tips of your fingers. This is a deeply unsatisfying handshake. You are left with the feeling that you both missed target – but neither one is brave enough to say, *"Shall we try that again!"*

In fact, we never tell people that they have screwed up a handshake. If you meet someone and he delivers an early handshake, you would never say, *"John, nice to meet you, but … what's up with your handshake?"*

Equally, we never own up to an error. If you accidentally deploy an early finger-squeeze handshake, you won't say, *"Gosh – sorry about that. Doesn't usually happen to me. Maybe I'm just tired!"*

Instead, we labour on and pretend it never happened – but the finely balanced scales just tipped slightly against us, the 50 per cent score just ticked down a notch. Not much, but enough to make things a little more tricky.

So, if you feel that maybe you have become stricken with ESS, correct it, next time, by going… all the way in and doing it properly.

STRENGTH

A soft, flimsy handshake is bad enough when delivered by a woman, but almost unacceptable from a man. Unless you have just left hospital having had a cast removed from a broken wrist and all your finger bones removed, there is no excuse for this! The rule is you should try to match strength. As the squeeze begins, gauge what's coming at you and meet it all the way. But don't go further; don't use your handshake to overpower or dominate. This might make you feel good, but will never encourage someone to engage in new business with you.

If you are male going to shake female, the odds are that the woman's hand will not be as strong as yours. So, as you apply pressure, again, match your strength to what's there. If you're a woman, don't feel the need to squeeze extra hard, but don't give up altogether with too dainty an offering.

BEAKING

Sometimes, ladies openly opt out of the usual handshake arena and offer up a hand formed into the shape of a bird's beak, almost like Her Majesty the Queen awaiting a bow and hand kiss. This "offering" states, somewhat bizarrely, *"Oh, yeah, it's okay. I don't shake hands like everyone else. I'm a lady, so I'm going to offer you this little beak shape to do with what you will."* Once again, there can be no excuse for this almost regal behaviour – it separates you from the crowd, in a peculiar way, and adds a strangeness to the first impression you make. The correct etiquette is to offer a flat palm so that hands touch properly.

CLEAN AND DRY

Men, yes, we do get sweaty palms. The wrong way to correct this is to wipe them down your jacket moments before shaking someone else's hand. Someone always sees you do it, and it doesn't even work! Instead, before any introductions are going to be made, go to the bathroom and rinse your hands off with cold water. The water both cools your hands down and acts like an astringent, effectively drying off your palms for a good 20 minutes.

If you have a drink in your hand, hold your cold, condensation-covered glass in your left hand, keeping your right hand dry in readiness for all those handshakes.

DON'T BE A BIOHAZARD

If you are in the middle of a coughing or sneezing fit and you have been using your hand to capture all those germs, do *not* offer it up for a handshake – no one will want it. If you persist in pursuing the handshake and the other person feels compelled through politeness to shake your possibly damp, germ-ridden hand, they could feel very uncomfortable. This will seal how they feel about you and your business for ever.

THE WRIST GRAB

While in the middle of a friendly handshake, don't also grab the other person's wrist with your free hand; it's tantamount to social kidnapping! The wrist grab displays "ownership" over the person you are grabbing onto and creates feelings of entrapment and inferiority in the other person. So, unless your intention is, in fact, to kidnap someone, avoid this gesture.

EYE CONTACT AND THE HANDSHAKE

It is essential to make eye contact with people as your hands connect. The same rule applies for when you clink wine glasses during a toast – to look away at the moment of the clink, it is said, can bring bad luck. I will always remember a TV producer in Manchester in the North of England who would always do the same thing every time he shook my hand. I would arrive at the studios to record the TV show and he would come down to

reception to greet me. He would reach out to shake my hand and, at the very instant of contact, he would look down, almost in shame or deference. This instantly demonstrated to me that, despite his title of "Producer", he clearly lacked confidence. By not being able to hold eye contact at the moment of the handshake, he was stating his lowliness. Incidentally, this matched his entire character. He rapidly lost control of the production team, the schedule and the budget. I'm not saying that had he made eye contact when he shook my hand things would have been vastly different – but my first impression of him was negative, and clearly so was everyone else's. He had a tough struggle from the start.

So, to summarize the handshake opportunity, if you can both exchange a firm, dry, satisfactory handshake with a clear beginning and a definite end, while maintaining eye contact throughout, what you are actually saying to each other is, *"Look how well we shake hands. Can you just imagine how good it would be to do business together?"*

MORE ON EYES

Eye contact is important during any conversation. It should be consistent and recurring, but not continuous. It should last long enough – several seconds – to prove that you are giving your attention to the other person, that you are interested, listening and absorbing what they are saying. It should not be a fixed, wide-eyed, glazed, unblinking, robotic stare that makes people uncomfortable, spooked or fear for their lives.

In general terms, you want to make eye contact when making or hearing:

- key points
- story highlights
- important details
- And, most importantly:

> **ALWAYS MAKE EYE CONTACT**
> **WHEN SAYING HELLO,**
> **GOODBYE OR SHAKING HANDS.**

READING THE EYES

The eyes are probably the single most expressive part of the face. Thus, if you are able to read some of the expressions made by people around you, this can give you a subtle advantage.

A slightly raised pair of brows indicates either interest or disbelief. A narrowing of the eyes can show empathy or disgust. A slow roll up of the eyes towards the heavens is an indicator that your audience has heard it all before and disagrees, or thinks you are talking outright rubbish! A widening of the eye combined with a single tilted nod of the head subtly directed at someone else in a meeting means *"I told you so."*

While you are talking in a meeting, if you see someone doing this wide-eyed head nod towards a colleague, you could infer that they had previously predicted what you were going to say, may have mentioned it as a theory themselves earlier, and indeed approve of it and are looking for agreement. So you can now appear super smart and say something like, *"This is probably something you have looked at yourselves, and here's why we think it will work …"* Your client will be dazzled by your mind-reading abilities and reassured that you are on the same wavelength: *"Wow, she really seems to know what I'm thinking and what we talk about – I trust her judgement, we should give her money."*

EYE MOVEMENT

This is something of a grey area, but experts tend to agree that the four key directions of eye movement when communicating – up, down, left and right – can have significant meaning.

If someone looks up before they answer a question, it can indicate that they have absolutely no idea what they are talking about: it's the equivalent of looking to the heavens for inspiration. If someone looks down before or during an answer, they are either shy, or lying, or worse – they could be a shy liar! None of those is good, so looking down should be avoided. It does seem to be acceptable, however, to look off to the side in order to gather your thoughts from time to time. It would look totally unnatural if, while you're trying to remember some statistics, you maintained a stony, unbroken death stare with your client.

Of course, this is an overly simplified look at a subtle and complicated subject, so I don't suggest you apply these interpretations religiously. But do at least be aware of yourself sufficiently to avoid perpetually looking down or up. And, as ever, be aware of the people around you, and what their eyes may be telling you.

THE GREETING KISS

There comes a point where your level of acquaintance with someone has risen to such a level that a handshake alone might appear too cold and distant. At that socially comfortable point, there is often the introduction of the greeting kiss. Usually between a man and a woman, this peck on the cheek accompanies a handshake and transmits a clear message to other colleagues and professional onlookers that, *"It's okay. We're not involved. We just know each other quite well and are keeping it professional."*

However, my friends, the hello kiss is fraught with danger and must be handled with care. Gentlemen, typically you lead with such a manoeuvre and must ensure that the lady in question is in no doubt about what you are doing and that you know how to pull it off successfully.

LEAN FORWARDS SLOWLY AND TO ONE SIDE

There is nothing more embarrassing than that painful, stilted moment where you both head towards the cheek kiss, but through a terrifying mismatch you simultaneously keep altering your head position as you get closer in a bid to avoid a full-on French kiss!

Control the situation by taking the lead. You tilt your head first, then slowly move in a curve, not directly ahead, towards the cheek you intend to kiss (hint: go for their left, your right). This steady and controlled approach sends out a clear, comfortable signal which is easy to read and avoids any bashing of noses, teeth and lips in a re-enactment of a scene from your teenage past!

ON THE WAY IN, BREATHE IN

All too often, people approaching this "business kiss" will be nervously talking, saying things such as *"So nice to see you"*, *"How have you been?"* and so forth. When you talk, you breathe out, and all that breath is flowing like a river of air directly into the face of the person you are about to kiss. Unless you are 100 per cent certain that your breath is as fragrant as a summer meadow, you may wish to avoid this approach. The solution is very simple. At the final approach, gently breathe in: this does mean shutting up for a moment (always a challenge for me!).

THE FIVE STAGES OF SUCCESSFUL NETWORKING

I want you to picture the early stages of any new relationship — whether business, social or romantic — as being established through the successful negotiation of these five hurdles:

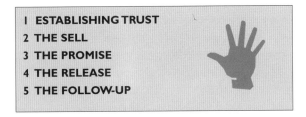

1 ESTABLISHING TRUST
2 THE SELL
3 THE PROMISE
4 THE RELEASE
5 THE FOLLOW-UP

ESTABLISHING TRUST

"Trust" is a big word, and can mean many things. Do you trust the babysitter not to pinch your DVD collection while you're out? Do you trust the advice of your new tax attorney? Do you trust your husband not to lie to you? In the context we're looking at here, we're dealing with the shallower end of the trust spectrum: we're not trying to get people you've just met to trust you with their lives, but to establish that you are genuine, sincere and worth getting to know further.

So in the world of networking, this is where you attempt to create a common bond. Do they know anyone you know? Have you worked with anyone they have? If not, can you create trust by convincing them of the quality of your current contacts? How about the work you do, the restaurants you eat at, where you live or go on vacation, the hobbies that interest you? Is there some common ground? Any of these areas could provide you with that essential link: a link to a positive feeling of trust and commonality.

THE SELL

This is where you employ your soft skills to sell your best features. You drop things into the conversation, without being too obvious or arrogant – but the message needs to be strong enough to be heard. It's also important that the sell is appropriate, relevant and interesting. Your "sell" should leave them impatient for more.

THE PROMISE

This is where you promise to call, email, text or get "your people to call their people" etc. It's a promise to form a relationship, however deep or shallow.

As part of the "promise", it always helps if you can offer up something of value in addition to that future call, maybe some information or another contact you have recommended. With the promise of a gift such as this, you not only engineer a new link, but also leave the recipient feeling as if they owe you something – always a good thing. Building up your payback credits like this (see chapter 1) is one of your key networking tools.

A great "promise" is where you suggest introducing your new contact to one of your existing contacts. The idea is that you are giving away something – something of value. Your existing contact will also be grateful, as you are also providing him with someone new and possibly beneficial. Both of these contacts, old and new, now feel as if they owe you a return favour. Great!

THE RELEASE

This is just another term for how to wrap up the conversation. Having exit strategies suitable for a variety of networking encounters is just as important as knowing how to engineer the introductions in the first place. Remember, last impressions need to be just as positive and memorable as first ones.

THE FOLLOW-UP

What good is a promise on which you don't deliver? There's nothing worse than the disappointment when a level of expectation has been created, but nothing happens. It's a bit like the *"I'll call you"* line after a one-night stand. Even if you decide after the initial encounter that this new contact is actually going to be of no use to you, still follow through with your follow-up. You will still be growing your network, always a valuable activity – who knows what referral they may make to you in six months' time?

We're now going to look at the first four of these stages in greater detail. The fifth, the follow-up, is covered fully in chapter 8, Leveraging Your Network.

Establishing Trust

FIRST IMPRESSIONS LAST
You get only one chance to make a first impression – it's an old saying, but it's more important today than ever.

You're sitting on a plane, a person you find offputting in some way is struggling down the aisle and, as they draw ever closer to that empty seat beside you, you start praying, *"Not me. Why is it always me? Please go and sit somewhere else."* But, of course, they end up sitting right next to you, breathing heavily, sweating slightly. You're now staring out of the window pretending they don't exist. By the end of this journey, however, you've actually spoken. He wasn't that bad and, in a funny way, even rather likeable.

The problem is that in the world of chance meetings and corporate networking, we rarely have the ability to hold someone captive for the duration of a plane journey – we don't get the opportunity to correct that bad first impression. We don't usually share the same tiny bottle of whisky and mini bag of pretzels, and as a result rarely get the chance to show off our full and wondrous personalities.

After all, would you have gone out of your way to talk to that offputting man if he was just standing next to you at a bar? No way. You'd have claimed your drink and walked off. In the real world, you have only a few seconds to make that good impression, which is why first impressions are so important.

WELL READ IS WELL FED

Part of your first-impression package is your image (see chapter 2), how you sound (see chapter 3), but also, of course, *what* you say. People will always be impressed with how intelligent, switched on and well informed you are, or at least appear to be! You can inspire people's confidence or trust in you when you display that you know what is going on in the wider world – that is, the world outside your own small but wonderful sphere. You don't want to come across as completely obsessed with only the minutiae of your own life.

You should be able to speak with some knowledge about economic news, political events and personalities, financial markets, industry trends, celebrity gossip and local developments. These are the conversational hooks that help to create connections with other people, and this is of course preparation you can do *before* the event itself.

Politics may well bore you to death, but you should still know what's going on. Don't worry; it's not about the detail. Just be able to skim over the surface of a story like a dragonfly over a pond and let others delight in filling in the details. It may go against the grain, but your job – when it comes to world and news affairs – is to know a little about a lot!

If, however, during conversation you admit to knowing nothing about the subject, you miss an opportunity to create a connection with the other person. If you are ignorant of a major news story, it can strike other people as odd, isolate you from them, and cause conversation to grind to a halt.

I remember sitting in a client's team meeting following the heavy Valentine's Day snowstorms across the northeastern United States in 2007. The following day, much of the news was dominated by a story about the unfortunate JetBlue aircraft that had sat on a New York runway for about six hours, causing huge delays and aggravation.

Initial warm-up conversation in the meeting covered the snowstorm. One of the team around the table mentioned the JetBlue incident. The CEO looked bewildered, admitted to not having heard of this event and wondered aloud why people chose to fly such an airline anyway.

What? How was it possible that this man had not heard this news? Had he, himself, been buried alive in the snowstorm? Clearly, it didn't materially matter one iota whether he had heard this major news or not; it did not affect his ability to do his job as CEO. But as polite, well-informed people in small-talk mode, the rest of us clearly found his remarks jarring. The conversation stuttered abruptly, and we quickly started on the business of the day.

Conversely, at a corporate dinner in Budapest, I was so impressed with a charismatic 60-year-old American man whose table I shared. He had wonderful insight into business and finance, but he also spoke with passion about travel, the political "machine", fashion and, most surprisingly, the TV show *Grey's Anatomy*. He recalled specific scenes that he loved and was able to engage with absolutely everyone around that table on many levels. That man demonstrated some of the finest communication skills that I have ever seen. His job? Head of a global tax practice!

Make it your business to learn about things that are nothing to do with your world. On top of "dragonfly-skimming" as many news/sports/entertainment websites that you can, find answers to questions such as:

- Who are today's in-demand fashion designers?
- What music are people listening to?
- What's the difference between Facebook and MySpace?
- Who hosts the top TV shows?
- Who won *American Idol/ The X-Factor*?
- Why is the interest rate so important?
- What is your major stock market doing and why?
- Who's in court/in jail/on top of the box office?
- When's the next election? Who's looking good to lead?
- When's New York/London Fashion Week?
- Where and what are people eating?
- What is funny on YouTube?
- What's the latest techno-gadget everyone's talking about?
- Who's making money/who's losing it?

And pick up publications that claim to be opinion leaders from *The Economist* and *Wall Street Journal* to *GQ*, *OK*, *US Weekly*, *People*, *Cosmo* and

Wallpaper. To prove yourself well informed, you have only to remember a few topical things from a range of subjects, and where you saw them, and the job is done.

DON'T LET ON!

If there are gaps in your knowledge – and something is bound to crop up in conversations with which you are unfamiliar – the trick is, don't give yourself away! An old theatrical saying is well worth remembering:

> **"THEY ONLY KNOW**
> **YOU'VE MADE A MISTAKE**
> **IF YOU ACT A MISTAKE."**

Never play up on your mistakes or knowledge gaps as you are advertising the fact that you've messed up. Instead, you should plead the Fifth Amendment (even if you are not a US citizen) and never incriminate yourself.

I'm not saying you should be dishonest or bluff your way through; someone who *does* know about the subject in question is bound to catch you out. But you can carefully disguise your ignorance with a few well-chosen phrases. Here are a few responses you can use when you have no idea what they are talking about, but you don't want them to know it!

For example, when asked whether you have heard of something or a certain someone: *"You know the author Malcolm Gladwell?" "Have you heard of Steve Jobs?", "What do you think about so and so …"* never answer with an outright negative, even if you've drawn a complete blank.

Instead say something like:

"I know I've heard of him, but remind me again."
"Ooh, tell me why I know that name."
"I know the name, but I can't remember why …"
"I think I read something about him recently."
Well, I have my thoughts, but tell me yours."

You've neatly glossed over the fact that you don't have much to say on this subject, and have turned it to your advantage by continuing to show interest in the opinions of your interlocutor and progressing the conversation. Make sure you listen carefully at this point; hopefully something they say will jog your memory or invite an interesting response of your own.

RESEARCH YOUR TARGET

This whole networking lark can appear a little cynical from time to time, and I won't deny it with regards to this next piece of advice. Sometimes, though, it's important to grab an opportunity to shine, make a connection or simply rise above the others. That's how you can become even more successful. The good news is that I have tested much of this out already so you don't have to!

So, try this. Before meeting up with key players in your life – or people you would like to become so – always do a tailored news search. Use the on-line search engines to find news that you believe could be of interest to the people whom you know you will be rubbing shoulders with at a forthcoming meeting.

On one warm spring morning in a somewhat featureless conference venue in Dallas, Texas, just before meeting a CEO client for a rehearsal, I did a search. I incorporated the letters "CEO" into the search – to see if any CEOs were in the headlines. Big news that I hadn't seen the previous evening was that the CEO of a major aircraft manufacturer had resigned/been asked to leave/used the emergency exit after an alleged indiscreet liaison.

I knew that the CEO whom I was about to meet would be aware of this news and so I made it my business within our small talk to ask if he had seen it. He had, naturally, and our conversation suddenly became very illuminated and animated as we shared thoughts on how awful the whole thing must have been.

I knew that this story would have reminded this particular CEO of the huge pressure of accountability that the role brings, and was able to incorporate that into the chat. Even better for me (albeit in a rather self-satisfied way), other members of the team who sidled up to become involved in what clearly looked like an interesting conversation had not heard the story and needed to be filled in. The CEO and I gladly delivered the gossip and scandal. That was a great connection moment, which would not have happened unless I had gone out of my way to find the information that I knew he would respond well to.

MAKING AN ENTRANCE

At any social or business gathering, particularly one that hasn't really got going yet, people are watching two things: their drink and the door. Let's leave the glasses of warm wine for a moment and talk instead about that all-important door. The big question is: are you interesting enough to warrant some attention?

So a big mistake at this crucial point of entry is to appear as bored – or boring! – as everyone else. Your mission is to look interesting and alert, to show by the way you enter the room that you have the potential to be a fresh, new and rewarding individual.

Remember, from the second you push open the door and enter the room, you are on show – you've just walked onto a stage. You can guarantee that most people will glance up to see who has just walked in. How do you look? Don't know? Move away from the door and walk calmly to the nearest bathroom. Check your appearance in the mirror and rinse your hands (to keep them dry for those all-important handshakes), then smile at yourself. Teeth okay? Good.

Right, back to the door … and you're in. Stand tall: imagine you are entering a competition where the tallest person wins – that's how tall you should act. A straight posture shows confidence, alertness and vitality; it also instantly pulls in your stomach and lengthens your neck (just in case you haven't lost those extra pounds yet). Appearing stooped over can seem resigned, defeated and submissive, in the same way as when your dog has wet the floor and shows his remorse by bowing his head and eventually rolling over for execution. Is that what you want to look like? An incontinent dog? Well, do you?! No, of course not – so tall it is. Having said that, it's got to be a "tall" that is consistent with your body – it shouldn't look strained or unnatural. Let's move on.

Start checking the room out. Who's here? Who's worth your time? Now clearly you shouldn't attempt this reconnaissance while talking to the boss's wife! Play it cool and gather intelligence as you proceed from one location to another, or while having a snack.

You spot someone you should talk to. Like a hunting animal, you must first bide your time; watch what is going on around your target. Let's assume it's a man. Start making judgements.

Is he alone and approachable? If so, in you go. Or does he look bored with the person he's talking to? Is he talking to a man or a woman? If it's a woman, I have got to be honest, you need to hold back a bit. Men like talking to women; it massages our egos. So wait a while until he starts to look bored or scan around the room. If it looks as if a conversation is ending, prepare to make your approach.

ONE-DEGREE NETWORKING

There is no better way to make a new contact than through someone you already know – in other words, by one degree of separation. Whether it's the bar or the boardroom, using a mutual acquaintance adds potency and implicit trustworthiness to your offering.

Let's say you're at a conference. Your friend/acquaintance is also present, and is chatting with someone who could be of great use to you. You approach and greet your friend, get introduced to your target and you're now part of this little group.

At this point, knowing what it is your target needs to hear (perhaps that you run an effective PR firm, you specialize in a certain type of dentistry, you are an IT specialist), you ensure that what you say to your friend broadcasts this attractive information. Even though at this stage you are addressing your friend, your message is laced with positive suggestions and information designed to pique the interest of the third party.

While delivering all this great content, knowing that you are being observed by your target, you should smile and nod regularly. This will create an additional air of positivity and will encourage your friend to do the same which, in turn, will persuade your target that you are clearly someone good to know!

The perceived "threat" level is low. Instead, because you are not selling directly to the target, the target can listen and come to their own conclusion – which is always far more powerful and effective – and they can be the one who asks to know more about you.

THE SELF-ENGINEERED INTRODUCTION

This is also known as the "who-do-you-know" method, and is a slight variation on one-degree networking. Engineer your own introductions to people wherever possible. Remember, if you don't ask, you don't get. So, ask people whom you already know who *they* know. If there's anyone among their contacts who could be of assistance to you or perhaps form the bridge to the target you really want to meet, then simply ask; the worst that can happen is that they can't help out.

For example, at a business event, large meeting or conference, go to the organizers (who just love being in control of this whole thing) and ask, *"So, who's here?"* They will be happy to point out people to you. *"Oh, there's Mr Harris. He runs that boutique software firm that they're all talking about. Oh, and there's Amy King. She's in charge of marketing communications at International Telecom …"*

This is great information. All that remains is to choose your moment and saunter over to said individual.

OPENING GAMBIT

All right, all systems are go and you are on your approach to your target. You arrive at the introduction zone. You should be positioned slightly more than an arm's length away from them; any closer is an invasion of personal space. If conversation goes well you can move closer, but never closer than an arms length – unless you want to kiss! Too many people breach that body zone, making the target feel uncomfortable and giving them way too much opportunity to smell your breath (which I hope you've ensured is mint fresh!)

Start the conversation with a polite smile and use the person's name straight away. That sounds weird, I know, but simply saying *"Hi, aren't you Amy King? I've been meaning to introduce myself/looking forward to meeting you ..."* is a whole lot better than piling straight in with your name and opening line. Referring to their name shows that you may have friends in common. And a name check always makes people feel a little bit more special: people love it when they appear to be known.

You are immediately going to get a smile and a yes from this person. You have demonstrated that she is known to you. She'll also be slightly worried by the possibility that she should know you. Now is the time to introduce yourself. Once you get to your name, that's when you offer your hand for the handshake (see pages 66-70).

Always have something else to say at this point. What could be more uncomfortable than if that's all you had to say then you just stood quietly next to her, staring at your drink? Try something like, *"Someone mentioned you were here and I was very interested to meet you. Communicating all the aspects of your company's product must be quite a challenge. How on earth do you prioritize?"*

Unless the situation has been horribly misjudged or, indeed, this is not Amy King (oops!), you have now initiated a conversation based on your target being interesting, powerful, successful and known. She likes it.

After detailing her business for a while, she will most likely ask what you do. You have been your own warm-up act and shown that you can listen. Now she will invite you to tell her something about yourself. You've reached the "sell" stage – well done! (See pages 87-92.)

TALKING TO TOTAL STRANGERS

What do you do if there is not someone around to introduce you to your target(s)? This can seem a bit more daunting, but remember, if nothing else, you have the fact that you are in the same place in common. And in establishing trust, it is identifying that initial common ground that gets you off to a flying start. Whether at a business or social event, you are obviously trusted as much as anyone else in the room by the people who have invited you to be there.

At weddings, the reason a person will sit and listen to another, or be more susceptible to being flirted with, is that, as guests of the wedding party, you are at least indirectly known and thus a more trustworthy quantity. "Oh, if you know him and I know her ... effectively ... we sort of already know each other."

There's a vast range of opening gambits to be played in these situations, depending on the occasion and setting. Comment on the food that they are eating or the music that is being played – something that is a shared experience between both of you at the time:

"How long does it take to get a drink?"
"Trust me, the shrimps are even better."
"Can you believe the view from here?"
"Last time I was in this boardroom, we were clinching the New York deal."
"How late is this bus going to be?"

– that's the kind of thing I mean. Once you've started up with one of these opening comments, your target is looking at you and waiting for more.

Another way to view any get-together is as a tangible version of the Internet. Everything you may need to generate business success is in that room. Each person is a website, but there's not much Googling going on. As a result, you have to research better and physically go visit the websites in the room. Do this with enough efficiency and you'll get to your ideal "site" and reach your target. (One difference with this "Internet" is that hopefully no one in the room will infect you with a virus or try to steal your credit card number!)

SIDLE UP AND EAVESDROP

This is another way to make initial contact with complete strangers. The sidle-up-and-eavesdrop approach is self-explanatory: you sidle up to two or three people and, while pretending to be doing something else, listen in on their conversation.

This approach is all about timing and knowledge. Timing because you can't randomly burst into a conversation and hope to be welcomed. No, you must wait for your moment, carefully balancing all the information you've heard until you think to yourself, *"Aha, now there's something I have some knowledge about and to which I can make a half-decent contribution!"*

This approach can work well on the dating scene. This is why bars where people stand around are infinitely better designed for dating and flirting than bars where everyone scurries off to some fancy seating. Once targets are sitting down, sidling up simply doesn't work – it looks like stalking!

HOW TO INTERRUPT

Creating the illusion that you are busy on your BlackBerry or smartphone, or have decided to, once again, check out the finger food, slowly gravitate towards your target group, and start listening.

In an ideal world, the conversation you are overhearing should be discursive. For example, if they are debating the relative merits of Apples over PCs, or whether *24* is better than *Lost,* you can politely interrupt and offer your view. Of course, if you've been really clever, you will already have identified your preferred target out of the group. Then, regardless of your own view, in this debate, you can side with that target, winning a new friend!

Two notoriously tricky topics you probably want to avoid in this initial approach are religion and politics. Calm and rational people can become really argumentative when discussing these two hot potatoes. As passionate as you may also feel about both these subjects, you have a 50:50 chance of either creating a friend for life or causing great offence. I don't know about you, but those are not odds that I would feel comfortable with.

Let's look at an example that may work:

TARGET 1: *"I tell you, interest rates are definitely on the rise again."*

TARGET 2 (your preferred target): *"I know you'd like to think so, but this is a flash in the pan – rates are moving down."*

TARGET 1: *"Inflation is already looking risky. Rates any lower than this and it will be out of control."*

TARGET 2: *"You can't believe statistics – just look at the high street, it's too quiet, the number of empty seats on flights. This economy needs to be encouraged …"*

YOU: *"Hi there, so sorry to interrupt,* [targets turn to look at you]. *Hope you don't mind being overheard but I happen to think that, while there may be a slight short-term risk of inflation, I would have to agree* [now looking at target 2] *that this economy needs just a bit of help, and frankly anything that gets the consumer out and about is good news for all of us."*

TARGET 2: *"Ha!* [looking at target 1] *See, I'm not alone thinking this way!* [turning to you]. *You're not an economist are you?"*

And off you go, a great chance for a self-introduction. Once in with this little pair, work fast. Let them know what you do, the sort of companies you work with and the people who you know, then release them first. Never allow them to be the ones to take a deep breath and say, *"Well, nice to meet you …"* No. You must get there first.

Now let's just be realistic for a moment. In the above example, you played things well, you judged timing right and it all progressed as planned. There is, however, always the slim chance that this little pair whose conversation you politely interrupted might turn around and tell you to sod off, get lost or be gone. If that happens, you smile as if unbothered (even though, inside you may be screaming with embarrassment) and wander off to a waiting getaway car! The fact of the matter, in this instance, is that you tried, and only by trying can you achieve your objectives.

Networking is a little uncomfortable, but when you occasionally leave your comfort zone, great things can happen.

(We'll be looking at how to end conversations a bit later.)

The Sell

Okay, so you've made initial contact, introduced yourself to your target and engaged in some small talk. But whether talking to a prospective client or potential date, there will come the stage where you need to sell yourself as someone the target really wants to know and stay in touch with.

Before we get stuck into how to make a good sell, I feel I really should clarify what a good sell is *not*. It is not simply an opportunity to boast about yourself, your qualifications, your most prized possessions, or whatever. Rather it is an opportunity to sell yourself subtly, conveying information tailored to your particular audience.

Here is an example of a sell that simply didn't work. I was hosting a major business network evening for financial directors in one of the smartest London hotels. The evening's main purpose was to do a soft sell to potential clients of the host company's products and services without them actually being mentioned. One of the representatives of this host company launched into his "sell" to a group of about eight people. What did he start telling us? A long, drawn-out story about him and his Ferrari. All right, we got the message: he owned a Ferrari. But the story went on and on. Worse, he noticed a few other people close by and drew them into the group. He updated them on his story, so, there it was all over again, him and his Ferrari. The net result of this 10 lost minutes was to be bored by a man who chose as his main selling point a car the value of which none of us particularly cared about, using a story which none of us found remotely funny. We laughed politely and drifted away.

He made several terrible social – not to mention networking – mistakes here:

Mistake 1: He dominated the group, preventing anyone else from speaking.

Mistake 2: He failed to notice our total lack of interest and our need to move on. He took so long on the (bad) sell that he didn't even get to the promise and release stages.

Mistake 3: He chose a completely inappropriate selling point. He actually put people off and thus lost all those potential new clients. If his audience had been college kids, young and hungry sales guys, or a couple of giggling 18-year-old girls, maybe he might have impressed someone. But among financial directors whose job is to root out and frown on excess while valuing profitable input, it was a disastrous choice.

The moral of this tale is threefold:

> 1 **KNOW YOUR AUDIENCE.**
> 2 **CHOOSE APPROPRIATE SELLING POINTS.**
> 3 **READ YOUR AUDIENCE'S REACTION, THEN RESPOND TO IT.**

I AM... A MOVIE TRAILER

A far better way to approach the sell is to think of yourself as a movie trailer. They always look good. I don't know about you, but I often end up preferring the trailers to the movie I've gone to see. So what does a trailer have that the movie often lacks? A trailer shows you the best bits, it drops a few clues, it teases you with who might do what with whom. There's great music, an exciting theme, a promise … it's coming soon. Quick, quick, get tickets. Someone make a note. I gotta see that one!

Now, the movie itself might end up being awful. But that doesn't matter, the sale was made. The movie company teased you with 30 seconds of foreplay to ensure you parted with your $12 to get you to go to see that movie. Done deal. Move on. Next.

This is what I want you to picture in your mind immediately before and during every new encounter. Ask yourself what you have that may be worth putting in your personal movie trailer. Maybe it's the fact that last year you worked with five of the top 10 companies in the world. Or perhaps you designed the most-used website in retail. Have a fact or two about each of your unique selling points ready to pull out whenever the opportunity arises.

PLANTING SEEDS

Whatever your unique selling points are, you need to transmit them to your target in an effective and subtle fashion, not pronounce them as bare factual statements. The more blatant you are, the more likely it will be that you sound as if you are showing off. The subtler you are, the more likely that your listener will enquire after some additional details.

It's the same for dating and flirting. Claim that you are the best kisser in the world, and your target will turn and walk. But mention that you happen to think that kissing is vastly underrated and that you think it is something very special, and you can guarantee that the person you are talking to will already be thinking about kissing you. The effect will be to convince your target that you are good while not having announced the fact. How else could you believe kissing to be very special unless you really were very good at it yourself? You're not asking for a kiss or forcing one on them. Instead, you are making them think about it and how good it might be.

Then just as you have their full attention and you can see that they are thinking about exactly what you have just been saying... change the subject and move on. It can be very effective. They might still turn and walk, but you will have got a lot further in their mind. You are using the power of suggestion (see pages 35–6).

In other words, you are planting seeds, not digging in 18-ft trees.

As part of your seed-planting operation in business networking, you need to ensure that your target knows that you work successfully with some pretty impressive players, clients or contacts. If you haven't been introduced by a mutual friend or contact, invoke recent successes and subtly drop in the name of a significant client (see below).

THE JEALOUSY REACTION

There is another psychological factor at work when successfully planting seeds in people's minds. It's known as the "jealousy reaction".

Imagine two children playing on the floor with a selection of toys. When one child picks up an as yet unused toy, the other child immediately reacts as if that were the only toy in the world, and now they must have it, too. Just seeing his little friend playing with a "new" toy provoked instant jealousy, and a screaming tantrum ensued. This jealousy reaction also operates in our adult lives, albeit hopefully without the tantrum. When we hear that somebody is benefiting from something that we have not yet used – we absolutely want to have a go, too … right now!

Here is an approach I took that incorporated planting some seeds, engineering a "jealousy reaction" and adding a dash of payback credit for god measure.

Recently I took the MD of a large consumer group to The Ivy in London for lunch. I had hosted many international events for him over the preceding months and wanted to encourage him to use some of my coaching programmes.

We sat down and enjoyed drinks and our first course. I was waiting for the conversation to turn around into what I had been up to. I then mentioned how a large law firm that was keen to win more business following a recent spate of lost opportunities had hired me to work with some of their senior partners. My story focused on the fact that this firm had somewhat bizarrely flown me all the way to Tokyo for just one partner, then back to London for everyone else. I knew, as I was telling the story, that some of his sales teams had also recently been losing business. I had guessed that he was already thinking of ways to improve the numbers. Suddenly there was I relating how I had not only guided senior lawyers in the art of winning business in a difficult sales environment, but was obviously considered good enough to be flown around the world for just one guy as well. At the end of my story, he got his organizer out and made a note. He said, *"I want you to email me with details of what you could do for us. It's something I had been thinking about anyway."*

He believed (partially correctly) that the idea of my coaching his salespeople had been his initiative. What actually happened was that my words triggered his reaction (just as I had intended them to). With his proposal that we work together, I knew my "sell" was complete. All I had to do now was keep the idea fresh in his mind and set the dates (see following up on pages 149–153).

NAME DROPPING

Another important element of the example above was that I had subtly yet clearly named the law firm with whom I was doing some effective business. But I didn't simply say, *"Hey, you know the magic-circle firm 'X' (I wish I could tell you, but I am SO not allowed!) uses me regularly. Maybe you should consider it as well."* This very obvious suggestion from me that he should employ me would have fallen on deaf ears. Instead, I dropped the name in passing while telling a story that was already highly relevant to my client. This particular client needed to hear that he would not be the first organization using me in this way, and knowing the name of this other client meant that he felt he was joining illustrious company. He had to come to the conclusion himself that, if a firm as well known as X trusted me and wanted to pay me money, he would be totally safe doing the same thing. My example created that same trusted link between the client sitting in front of me and the law firm with whom I had just worked, and they didn't even need to talk to each other!

The lesson here is to do your research, to fully anticipate and understand what your target needs. After that, using subtle language, you need to demonstrate ways you could fulfil those needs just as you are already doing for others – creating the jealousy reaction.

The Promise

The promise is all about bringing the relationship into a full-fledged form. It's about your promises to your target, not the other way around. The purpose of the promise – apart from the promise itself – is to disarm your target by making no demands of your own. There is nothing less effective than, on your first meeting with someone whom you could do business with, attempting to force a decision there and then.

Let's say you sell BMW cars for a living. You meet someone at a function who expresses an interest: *"I've always wanted to drive one of those 7 series cars."* It's a great lead-in, probably more than you would usually get. But don't jump at it – do not be tempted to see this invite as a guaranteed sale, if only you just push a bit further. Don't start trying to establish a date for the test drive, how much they would pay and whether they would like you to arrange a finance package. No, too much too fast! The target will suddenly take fright and, despite quite fancying a test drive, now declines altogether and makes his excuses. Lost him, damn!

The correct way to deal with any initial expression of interest is simply to continue the game. Swap contact details in a relaxed "don't-worry-I'm-in-no-rush" type of way, and promise to follow up. It may be fast approaching the end of the financial quarter and you really need the numbers, but you do not let that show. The cooler you play it, the more persuasive and genuine you will appear. Clients can smell desperation.

Offer up some "We coulds…", such as *"We could think about arranging a test drive for you,"* or *"Next week, we could fix an afternoon for you to come and wander round the showroom some time."* Or *"If you like, I can connect you with some current owners and you can get their opinions."* None of these choices has any teeth; they don't force an immediate decision or commitment. He is far more likely to agree to think about coming down to the showroom than to sign a finance agreement while still holding his glass of wine.

You are not looking to exit any networking situation with the business already done, the contract already signed. Rather, you want to open a door and prop it open until you do your follow-up.

THE COLUMBO METHOD

Columbo, that old TV detective, would question a suspect for a while and then appear to finish. But, just as he was exiting the room, he would turn around and say, *"Oh, just one more thing."* The suspect was suddenly off guard and could possibly incriminate himself.

Now you're not trying to get your target to admit any deep, dark secrets. But you can employ the same method: allow your target to see that you're about to leave. What little guard is left comes down, and you can strike with your "promise proposal". There are dos and don'ts for this as well. Don't use the promise to force the acceptance of an invitation.

Don't say: *"Would you like to meet for drinks next week?"*
His reply may well come back: *"I can't. I've got meetings in Seattle."*

Then you're forced into either saying, *"Oh."* – or appearing desperate and pleading: *"What about the next week, or the next, or the next …"*
Game over.

Instead, be professional and cool: *"Here's what I'm going to do. I'll call you in a couple of days, and let's stay in touch."*
Or: *"Let me email you some dates, and we can pick a good one for drinks."*

You're not asking for a decision right now. You are not even asking a yes or no question; you are simply flagging up that your email or call is on its way. There's no pressure on your target, everyone is happy. Easy!

The Release

Throughout the entire encounter with your target, keep evaluating how you are doing – whether you have peaked or he has had enough. This is where you must consider an early release. There is nothing more dreaded in a social gathering than being trapped by a bore – remember the mistakes made by the Ferrari guy (see page 88). Once this has occurred, you automatically lose any further chance to engage the target in conversation. Your aim is to have established trust, done your "sell", and suggested your "promise" – all before the target has lost interest. You want to leave them wanting more, not sighing in relief at getting away. It's a question of good timing: making your excuses and moving on before your target does the same. It's a race to a very fine line. The winner is the one who reads it right and walks away strong.

RELEASING TOO LATE

I don't want to sound like a broken record, but you have to stay aware of the reactions of the person you're talking to. If your target makes any of the following signals, you've gone probably gone on too long and your release could be too late:

He suddenly folds his arms – He is putting up a barrier between you and him.
He checks his watch – He's wondering how much time has elapsed and how much is left.
He takes a really deep breath – He would like to say *"Anyway, I'd better be off as I'm really bored now."*
He sees someone else and makes sure they see him – Let's face facts: he wants to go and talk to them. He could even be appealing to be rescued.

If you spot one of these signs and react promptly, you can still salvage the situation (see Getting It Right, below). But if you don't, the next time he sees you, this person won't remember how cool and clever you are. Oh, no. He'll remember the amount of time and effort it took to prise himself away from you so that he could go where he wanted. He may well seek to avoid you in the future.

CLOSING THE CIRCLE

A great way to end a conversation is to come full circle – mention something the person said much earlier. This demonstrates that you have been listening and that you have a witty knack of drawing thoughts together. For example if, during a trade event, you mentioned how, when travelling, you communicated with your kids by webcam and your target had shown interest, you could use that. No doubt conversation will have moved on, but once you are ready to release him first you say, *"Well, I'd better let you get on and look around the stands here, and, by the way, if you decide to check out webcams, I have found Logitech to be pretty good ..."* And, with a neat exit comment and some useful guidance, you have released your target and you are away!

MAKING YOUR EXIT

Finally, make your farewell and leave. The mere fact of your moving on creates the impression that you are not a lonely soul with no one else to talk to, but a busy and confident person who is good to know, and keen to know lots of other people.

Important note: On exit, keep walking. Don't take three steps and, in full view of the people you've just left, start searching the room for your next target. This could well imply that actually *you* were the one who grew bored and that your excuse for leaving was insincere, and could well cause offence. Go get some air, head for the bathroom, return to the organizer's desk or check your BlackBerry.

In the same way as if you were chatting up someone, then saw an even more attractive person and broke off hurriedly to approach this second target, don't be tempted to start a new business conquest while in the middle of the current one – you don't want to appear to be an NS ("networking slut")!

THE DATING EXIT

Having met and clearly fascinated this wonderful person at a bar, you need to follow exactly the same rules regarding your exit. Like a great comedian, you want to leave while things are going really well to create that need in them to see you again. Make sure you have each other's contact details and announce that you will be in touch. Smile, say goodbye to any of their friends, then, like a phantom, you're gone! This confident disappearing act of yours will build up huge anticipation before the first date. Once again, despite how well everything just went and how confident you now are, do not attempt to double up and start the same activity with somebody else. This bar is done – time to move on home or somewhere else.

GETTING IT RIGHT

You know you're getting it right if the final exchanges in your networking conversations go something like this:

IMPORTANT EXECUTIVE: *"Yes, well, that certainly sounds interesting."* (Oh, dear, he's checked his watch, or gestured to someone else over your shoulder with a "hello" wave. He might even have taken a deeper-than-usual breath.)

YOU (You saw his signals and are smart enough to respond promptly, well done): *"It was really good to meet you. Here is my card and I have your details. I tell you what, I'll email your PA with some potential dates for a meeting and I could pop in with some of those ideas."*

IMPORTANT EXECUTIVE: *"No problem. She's called Sarah. Have a good evening."* (You're shaking his hand. Nice!)

This man will remember this as a pleasant and productive encounter with you. He won't be concerned for his freedom should the chance arise for another chat. He's expecting your email. And, as a bonus, you know his PA's name and suddenly you're in. Very impressive!

Travel Networking

WHY IT PAYS TO FLY IN STYLE
They say you have to speculate to accumulate. When it comes to travel, spending a little more can often result in extra results over and above the luxury accommodation. Despite all protestations to the contrary, the United Kingdom still operates on a well-defined class system. In the United States, it doesn't exist as clearly... unless you are flying.

Once there is a big plane involved, we all split ourselves into classes. Oh, sure, it may be driven entirely by financial consideration – I mean, why pay $1,650 for a round trip to Vegas when you can hop on Jetblue and pay $117. It's all to do with placing yourself in the best company and using your environment to sell yourself.

When you settle into your big comfy leather chair in the second row of first or business class, the person next to you will make an immediate assumption: *"He's one of us."*

He'll also be thinking, "Hey, I wonder what this guy does to earn enough money or clout to get himself in this pricey seat like me ... probably something good." Your neighbour now sees you as a potential equal. Now that you have placed yourself in his "class", he is making all sorts of good assumptions about you: you have placed yourself in his zone of trust.

In England, gentlemen of a certain position in life often join (or are invited to join) a posh city gentlemen's club. You can't just saunter into these places. Oh, no. It's all whispers, rumours, handshakes, invites, nods, contacts and networks. But once you are in, you become part of an exclusive clique. Part of the gang. Suddenly a lot of business is done, deals are made and networks continue to be built up.

The equality of the gentlemen's club membership removes the barriers that would otherwise be in place. Before membership, these people – through their different social and business spheres of activity – may never otherwise meet or do business together. Once part of the membership tier, it's all laughs, handshakes and *"Well, if you're good enough to get in here, old chap, you're good enough to marry my daughter or join my board. Cigars and port all round."*

Obviously, it's a somewhat different dynamic on board a 747-400, but, still, that same conclusion is drawn: you have given yourself a certain exclusivity and marked yourself as a person of quality. Passenger A, sipping Champagne next to passenger B also quaffing bubbly, is suddenly in the same group. There is no reason a conversation can't start up. The playing field has been levelled, and you are to be listened to as much as anyone else in their exclusive circle.

THE BARRIERS ARE DOWN

When people travel or eat or go on vacation – in other words, when they are away from the office – their barriers come down and you have a far better chance to make useful contact with someone than through the usual methods. Around a swimming pool with your shorts on and kids running around shrieking, firm friends are made out of total strangers. Phone that same stranger while he's dressed in his business suit in his office, guarded by his PA, and he doesn't come to the phone: the barriers are up!

Imagine the scene. You are lining up to board the flight from New York to London. Oh, my God – it's only the finance director of the hottest retailer on the planet, right in front of you. As the seemingly endless wait to board goes on, you strike up a conversation. You both get your boarding pass checked simultaneously and you walk together to the door of the plane. Oh dear, they turn left and are immediately swept up into the warm embrace and the soft beds of first and business class. You, with your budget in mind, are off to the farm — the cattle farm. Shuffle to the right, sir. Conversation over.

Yes, fair enough, it doesn't always work this way. However, the image of success is a powerful one. At the beginning of my career in communications, I made many trips from London to the United States, and I won a great many deals and contacts by always flying in business class. People talk; they exchange cards. Business gets done.

Only recently I was sitting next to this guy of a similar age to me. He smiled politely as he sat on the seat next to mine. Then he got out his laptop, a newspaper and put his phone away. I wasn't angling for a new contact — I wanted to work on an event script I was writing — but I noticed that he started playing that numbers game Sudoku. I gestured over to it and said in a relaxed friendly tone, *"If you start that now, you'll get nothing else done."* This created an atmosphere of ease and familiarity.

He looked up and smiled, *"You're not wrong, but I've challenged myself to complete one before we take off."* I wished him luck and returned to my work. This was an ideal situation as it was something that I could follow up on later, which was exactly what I did. We got chatting about the game, then about what we both did. There were drinks being served and a friendly non-threatening, non-business-like atmosphere. After I explained what I did (expertly planting my seeds!) I left him alone again.

Later, he sparked up a further chat. *"You know I was thinking about what you said, I reckon our people could do with some of that. Give me your card and let's have a chat once I get back to London."*

That one flight has resulted in more than $15,000 worth of business.

Flying "up front" I have met CEOs, directors of finance, a couple of movie stars and one former prime minister of Great Britain (that was pretty cool!). Yes, you're right, sometimes you will meet absolutely no one. But the chances of meeting someone who could, at some stage, provide an income stream are far higher in the front of the plane than at the back. Yes, it costs more … but … no pain, no gain!

In any case, there is no longer any need to pay full price or rack rate for your airfares. There are many clever and smart travel consultants out there who know the deals and can get you into business class for a coach fare. Just search for them and never divulge your secret.

If you do a lot of transatlantic voyaging like I do, I can truly vouch for the type of business acceptance you get in the first-class lounge or top seats of the excellent Virgin Atlantic or the dignified British Airways First service, not forgetting the super new all-business-class airlines such as Eos and Silverjet (not withstanding recessionary pressures on their ability to survive!)

So, if you get a chance to travel anywhere on business, always take it – don't bail because you had drinks planned with friends or because you don't think it's worth your time. Every journey represents a golden opportunity for you to meet potentially valuable contacts. Take my word for it. Upgrade yourself, and upgrade your chances in business networking.

IN SUMMARY, AS LONG AS:

- you don't have spinach stuck on your teeth…

- you stand tall and business-like…

- you have a confident introduction and a firm, dry handshake that says "I'm worth dealing with"…

- you keep what you have to say focused and brief…

- you name-drop a bit and you use the right type of sell…

- you offer an enticing promise and release first…

… you will be networking your way to success.

CHAPTER 5

Going Up?
Your Elevator Pitch

We've already explored a lot of communication skills in the previous chapter on networking. In this chapter, we are going to explore further a niche "sell" stage (see chapter 4) of your soft-skills arsenal – this time, not in a large, sociable gathering, but in any random encounter in which you have no introduction, and probably have only a minute or two to make an impression – the elevator pitch.

First we better define what exactly an "elevator pitch" is. The elevator pitch is, in effect, your answer to the question, *"So, what do you do?"* The idea is that, in the time it takes an average elevator to reach the floor where you might get off, you have been able to explain briefly to someone what you do, why you are so good at it, the value and benefits of what you offer and why this stranger should be interested in using you or at least referring you to people who might need your talents.

It's a tall order. On average, 30 seconds is the target time for your ideal pitch. Not only is this achievable, but actually it's essential as well – at its best it will open the doors of interest to you and what you offer. It is a useful way of marketing yourself. In effect, when you deliver an elevator pitch, you are performing your personal TV advert – a commercial displaying your wares and enticing people into your world.

Let's set aside the fact that few people speak to each other in an elevator. In fact, vertical conversations are sometimes the reserve of the insane or drunk. For the rest of us, we stare ahead in morbid fascination at the numbers increasing or declining, wondering why it is taking so damn long.

Even more of us, it turns out, play the "door close" game. You know what I mean. You rush into an empty elevator, push your floor button and wait for the lethargic snail-pace doors to close. It's at that point that you notice some panting individual racing for your elevator – as if there aren't another five to choose from. He has spotted you and visually appealed for you to hold the lift. You create the illusion of fumbling for the door-open button, while you are actually furiously pressing the door-close button. (This button serves no purpose by the way. It's a trick button.)

With luck, the doors close in his face, while you appear to have been trying your best to open them, and shrug your shoulders at him as he disappears from view. Ah, well, you'll never see him again!!

But, given that the gods are against you and the doors stay open, he makes it in and bizarrely starts talking to you! You need to be ready for the fact that this guy might actually be important.

PREPARING YOUR PITCH

Actually, the creation of your elevator pitch is a great exercise in examining for yourself what you do, what truly matters and which bits are worth communicating to anyone who might listen. Consider it a verbal identity-edit, cutting out the irrelevant bits and retaining the essentials that truly define what you are about. And making it all sound interesting and appealing in the process! It helps you to review and define what it is you do, what you stand for and who you are. You'll be stunned by how many people aren't really sure about some of those seemingly basic facts and are simply unable to communicate effectively what it is that they actually do.

It is also a fine way to become more adept at delivering brevity. Don't forget – every time you hold someone's attention for less time than they had anticipated, you are giving them the gift of time. A gift of great value and one you should generously hand out each and every day. People like being released early, they will always be grateful (see pages 94–7).

Take some time out to see if you can explain to yourself what you do, then make it sound even better. I want you so excited by your description of what you do that you feel a new-found thrill at the prospect of going in to work on Monday morning. Lead with this… and the success will follow.

What are the rules of the perfect elevator pitch?

THE OPENING STATEMENT – A SHOCKER!

A great tip given to me by a talented Canadian communications expert, Jason Thomson, is to say something arresting, almost shocking, in order to keep the listener listening. Ideally, this short, initial comment should contain no more than six or seven words.

The opening question might be as simple as, *"So, what is it you do?"*

And your pitch begins...

"I make dreams come true" (cosmetic surgeon) or *"I create success"* (financial director) or *"I turn impossible visions into perfect buildings"* (architect) or *"I try to explain the world to the world"* (journalist) or *"I bring order to chaos"* (IT developer).

You get the picture. Bold, arresting statements that encourage curiosity and a need to know a little more.

You may, at this stage, feel like relaxing back with a smug smile and completely give up on any further explanation. This would be a mistake, as you would simply appear to be an idiot – very much like the idiot I once met at a dinner event who "hilariously" introduced himself as a professional football player. He was about 43 and thought that he was the "life and soul" of any party. To be more accurate, he was that embarrassing soul that most people tried to ignore.

You don't want to be like him. So, continue with...

THE PYRAMID APPROACH

After successfully deploying your opening salvo, you now need to shift to the pyramid approach. Starting at that pointy apex, you have delivered your brief opening statement. You need to broaden your pitch in two or three further stages enabling you to reach the base of the pyramid and the conclusion of your elevator pitch.

Your opening statement has been intriguing enough that virtually anyone should want to know more. You want to widen your approach, give it a bit more definition, and add relevant content that should trigger the "I need this person" reaction.

Each statement should build on and contribute interest to the previous statement. Each stage moves you closer towards making a new contact, winning a new client.

Let's say you are a fitness trainer and most of your work is for big companies based in the financial district; you have some great corporate and individual relationships. In addition to the fitness, running and resistance training, you give out nutrition advice as well. You regularly write interesting newsletters with tips and advice for your clients, and there's enough business to keep you busy for three days a week.

- **Your opening statement:**
  "I make bodies look good naked!" – your pyramid's apex.
  Purpose: Intrigue your listener.
  Intended response: *OK, I have to know more!*

- **First pyramid level:**
  "I'm a high-level fitness trainer for winners in the corporate sector."
  Purpose: There's your slightly wider pyramid level – a great start to explaining the nature of what you do, your category, what you offer and the sort of people who use your services.
  Intended response: *I still don't know how it works, and I find myself wanting to know how you positioned yourself in this specialized and presumably rewarding sector.*

- **Second pyramid level:**
  "I work closely and personally with financiers on their fitness, image and health."
  Purpose: You've broadened it further, defining several things you can offer.
  Intended response: *OK, I now know that you build close relationships with people. They must value and trust you to let you in that close. I might be interested in health, fitness or image, and you have ensured that you mention them all to spread the net of potential a little wider.*

- **Third pyramid level:** *"Together we create an intense plan for food, workouts and lifestyle, and I guide or push to get success every time."*

  Purpose: You've offered some details about what you do and a statement about your dedication to the job. You've made a focused and precise statement; you've reached the base of the pyramid.

  Intended response: *You are showing me that you are a team player. It's not just you, but rather you and others that create these plans. You are flexible enough to explain that in some instances you are not afraid to push people to achieve their objectives and at other times gentle guidance will be your contribution. You are confident in what you do and imply that it works every time. I might not believe absolutely everything you say, but... I'm going to hire you because I want the fitness success that you seem to understand.)*

MATCHING THE PITCH TO THE PERSON

Let's keep the above example going a while longer. What if the person is already fit and strong-looking? You would be best advised to refer to "continued success" or "reaching the next level".

What if the person is a bit of a weighty and out-of-breath individual? You should talk about the importance of those initial steps, how hard it can be – the first time on those gym machines – and the secrets of eating to lose weight and how it heralds the start of a new life. Lots of enticement, promise and potential.

> THE SMARTEST PITCHES CONTAIN A CORE OF FACTUAL INFORMATION, SURROUNDED BY A FLEXIBLE, DYNAMIC SET OF "SELL IDEAS" THAT CAN BE PICKED, MIXED, REORDERED AND LAID OUT TO APPEAL IN EXACTLY THE RIGHT WAY, TO THE RIGHT PERSON, AT THE RIGHT TIME.

Sometimes it makes sense to jump straight in and reveal your pitch at the earliest opportunity. On other occasions it is better to hold back a little, gather some essential data first, then reveal your pitch in a way that will directly appeal to the target.

On a recent vacation in Santa Barbara, I met a lawyer from a firm with which I had never had any contact. I decided to wait for him to tell me all about his world before revealing mine. I soon learned that this guy had left his firm, only to return, and was now on a fast track to the desired status of anyone involved in law – becoming a partner. Once you reach partner status in a law firm, your earnings can skyrocket, and your future is pretty much secure. To my knowledge, people in this position have to start acting differently to ensure that the deciding body sees them as fitting the bill, from an earnings and client-relationship position, and as the right "kind" of person. Law-firm partnership is like a private club: they vote you in or blackball you out.

I realized that he was at the stage of his career when he had to ensure that his image, communication and message were consistent with someone who would comfortably be selected as a new partner with this top-ten firm.

When it was time for me to say what I did, I simply used my standard pitch about helping organizations and individuals attain more success through smarter communication, networking and soft skills, but added that I often worked with senior partners, newly promoted associates and CEOs looking to improve their impact on shareholders, colleagues and clients. That last statement was what struck a chord.

His response was exactly the result I was after: *"I must get your card before you leave."* Excellent.

Spend time on your elevator pitch. Write down all of the things that you do, are responsible for, are proud of or hope to achieve, and work it into a pyramid of opportunity. Sometimes that 30-second shot can change your life and lead you in new and wonderful directions.

Having a flexible elevator pitch is a sign of preparation, confidence and readiness.

When someone asks you what you do, it is a wonderful opportunity to sell your brilliance or, at the very least, hone, perfect and fine-tune your message ready for the next time.

More than this, though, throughout my time coaching teams and individuals in the world's largest companies, organizations and groups, I have found that possessing the ability to effectively describe and passionately explain what you do in a way that drives people's interest and enthusiasm is a huge advantage. You owe it to yourself to be ready to deliver that pitch!

CHAPTER 6

Meeting and Boardroom Etiquette

> Despite the new air of confidence you have acquired
> – through using the soft skills you have learned in the
> previous chapters – the boardroom can still be one of
> the most demanding and intimidating "arenas of
> communication" in which you'll ever sit. (Please note
> that in this chapter I will be referring to a full-size
> boardroom, but all the ideas and considerations that
> follow apply equally well in any-size meeting room
> or, indeed, any informal business group.)

It's just a room with a big expensive table, a nice view and a whole bunch of chairs, right? Sadly not. The boardroom is a court of opinion, a sobering venue for expression and judgement; it's a theatre where your performance is about to be judged; it's a living blog – your comments available for all to immediately challenge or welcome; it's a venue in which to be seen and heard ... or not; it's the place where reputations are made and broken.

This is the arena where you prove what you are worth. Of course, you're already doing that outside the boardroom – in your day-to-day work, exploiting your business relationships, signing contracts and closing huge deals, right? Well, yes ... but in the boardroom there is a difference – everyone is watching you at the same time ... and you are centre stage. The boardroom or meeting room can be compared to performing on live TV. Your job? To ensure that no one wants to change the channel.

WHY IS IT SO IMPORTANT?

Your boardroom appearance is a rare opportunity to impress a great many more people than you would usually have access to – people who may well be placed to help you up the ladder.

You should always seek to expose yourself to these sometimes uncomfortable opportunities. Every time you appear – every time that you get some "stage time" – you grow your brand and you build your network, your power and your effectiveness.

Naturally, with any "brand grab" such as this, there is inherent risk. What happens if you blab a load of inappropriate garbage? Or, after 10 minutes of the finest monologue you can create, the others just lean back and laugh at you? What if your ideas are shot down in flames or you sound like an idiot?

There are risks associated with pretty much everything we do. Stepping out of the front door in the morning could result in you being hit by a bus or savaged by a confused antelope, but you still go out. If you desire success, risk is something you should welcome. It is only by taking personal risks that you grow and meet with the opportunities that allow you to succeed.

It's often the case in these risky moments that, as you are observed by the great and the good in your world, you can change and influence the very nature of your future success. This is when you get access to enough people to create your own mini "tipping point". If you manage to convince 10 colleagues or clients within a meeting that you have the qualities they desire, word will spread and, before long, good things will start to happen.

The way that you play the boardroom is crucial. Ignore the soft-skills rules and blunder your way through, and you could be left ruing the day you accepted the invitation to the meeting. Stick to the rules and understand the game, and you will shine in those big meetings. It will be only a matter of time before more golden opportunities are laid at your feet.

Before we push open those smart double doors and stride confidently into that open arena, let's look at a few basic rules.

PLAYING THE PART

I know what you are thinking: *"Oh come on, I've attended a zillion meetings. I know what I'm doing, I'm gonna skip this bit."* Well, stop right there!

In my world of high-level coaching, I often meet people who believe they have the whole thing "down", who think they are in control of a situation and yet, tragically, are not. They believe that what they have to say is truly useful to all around that table and that their control of time and agenda is impressive. The problem in business is that, all too often, nobody puts these people right when they get it wrong. No one takes them to one side after the meeting is over and says, *"Hey, not bad in there, but most people were bored rigid and you have quite an arrogant tone – plus, you never listen. Other than that … er … you'll probably get fired soon."*

This problem can become increasingly embedded the more senior you become. Many upper-level players surround themselves (often unwittingly) with "yes" people. These are peons who are too concerned about their own jobs to ever openly criticize their boss, who say yes to every question and relentlessly offer praise like a gushing fountain of reassurance! Of course, these people are actually doing a disservice to their employer by never helping them to see the error of their ways and as a result never enabling it to be corrected. The truly smart leaders demand to know their mistakes so that they can continually refine their game. Unfortunately, not all of them do.

To ease your way into being a great adviser and confidant, you should offer up "observations" and "suggestions" as a choice:

"If you think it may help, I have some observations that may help you further to refine your style."

Rather than:

"Good Lord, you were bad – a chimp could do better than that!"

There now follows an array of suggestions for your meeting experience; choose which elements work for you – remember, it's your tool kit.

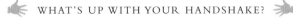

WHO HAVE YOU COME AS?

Looking the part is all about your overall image (see chapter 2). Yes, it's your outfit – the smart, appropriate clothing of someone going somewhere. But it's much more than that. It's also your attitude and your conscious awareness of the image that you are communicating. Which role are you going to assume? What attitudes are you going to convey?

- Team player?
- One of the boys?
- Future leader?
- Woman with a mission?
- Not interested?
- Ideas man?
- Image isn't as important as my talent?
- Would rather be somewhere else?
- Don't understand any of this?
- Sexy chick?
- Woman trying to be a man?
- Someone different enough to be interesting?

Your image significantly contributes to your entire impact – your presence, how people interpret the message constantly streaming off you. It covers how you walk through the door, where you choose to sit, how you appear within the meeting, how you listen, where you look and so forth.

If you are not thinking about how others perceive you, if you have not pre-planned the conclusion that you want them to come to about you in that meeting, then you are not properly prepared. You have to be consistent with your character and personality, but if you know that your true strength and intended direction is leadership, then you need to display this within the meeting.

So, let us enter this mahogany land of opportunity, replete with its forests of fancy chairs, coffee-flavoured beverages, overhead projectors, curly sandwiches and completely ineffective temperature controls.

WHAT TIME IS IT?

It's late, that's what time it is. By ALWAYS assuming you are late, you will always be on time – at least, that's the idea. There is nothing worse than arriving at any meeting late. It gives *such* a bad impression.

First, you will look sweaty and stressed and frustrated. If you are late, this is usually a deliberate performance to show people that it was not your fault and that somehow you were held up against your will – trains, sick cat, kids, weather, or a combination of factors – and that you had to race against time to make it. Secondly, if you were nonchalantly to stroll into a meeting late it would demonstrate the height of rudeness, or, at the very least, a complete inability to follow a schedule. So, a frazzled look it is.

Arriving late will also put you at an immediate disadvantage, from which you might not recover, even by the end of the meeting. You would have missed out on any introductions and small talk, and you would have no clue as to what had already been covered and what had not.

The moral of this tale is: do *not* be late! Check the time of your meeting, work out how long it will take to get there, then add half an hour. If that means that you do indeed arrive too early, go and sit in a coffee shop and try to figure out how much money they must take in an hour!

TAKE A SEAT ... BUT WHERE?

If there are windows in the room, it is always advisable to sit at the table facing those windows. This way, the people you are addressing will sit opposite you and not be distracted by fancy helicopters, dog-shaped clouds or rare birds flapping around outside. The last thing you want while delivering your key points in your effective and winning style is your client or employer staring over your shoulder out of the window and suddenly shouting, "*Hey, everyone, look, a helicopter! Wow, wonder where it's going ...*"

More importantly, they won't be dazzled by the bright outdoor light flooding in behind you. Irrespective of how good you look, if you have your back to the windows it makes it generally less comfortable to look in your direction, and on a sunny day people may have to spend the afternoon squinting at you. A backlit condition, as any photographer will tell you, is never the best way to view an image of any sort.

So, switch it around – you should face the windows.

You are a professional, you can take the discomfort of sitting in this frontlit situation because you now know that you will be looking great – you have natural daylight flooding your face, creating a fresh and bright-eyed appearance, which will improve the impact of your message.

Back in my TV production days, I worked with one British actress – a complete diva – who insisted that everywhere we went, if she were to do a spoken piece to camera or be filmed in any way, she would dictate the position of the lights. Every time, without fail, she would insist that they were lowered from their standard height right down to face level. Sure, this was extra work for the crew and, as any good crew would, they mumbled their discontent. But, you know what, she was always right. She always looked better.

In television you learn the ultra-importance of lighting. Trust me, I know what I'm talking about! In fact – without wishing to turn you into a paranoid lighting freak too anxious to sit down anywhere – you should also try to avoid sitting directly underneath those low-voltage but very bright halogen lights that cast an intense downward light beam. Like a *Star Trek* phaser, it will slice through your face, creating one of those sinister Night Of The Living Dead effects – the sort you created as a kid with a flashlight under your chin, but in reverse. Okay, I know that now you are going to be acting a little odd as you shuffle your chair left a bit, right a bit, to avoid the shaft of mega-light turning your eyes into blacked-out hollows – but you'll thank me!

And finally, if any helicopters were to fly past the window (a worrying event if you are on the ground floor), you must naturally resist the temptation to be distracted yourself.

THE DOOR

In addition to thinking about the position of you, your client and the window, you should try to avoid sitting down with your back to the door.

When sitting facing or to one side of the door, you have ample time to see and acknowledge who is coming in. You can calmly and coolly stand up in time for a well-executed handshake (remember, match strength, a couple of seconds or so, retain eye contact – see chapter 4). Take care not to stretch wildly across the expanse of that great mahogany slab and fall onto the table, sending coffee flying in all directions. Instead, simply walk around to greet people.

With your back to the door, you are always the last to know who has just walked in, always the slowest to stand and, as you push the chair back, you also run the risk of ramming it into the person who has just walked in or indeed tripping him up over it. Plus you will be the first to be murdered as you will always be the last one to notice that an axe-wielding madman has just entered the meeting room. Ha!

I learned while on a job in Tokyo recently that it is traditionally considered good etiquette to seat clients facing the door to give them the best chance of survival if anything untoward happen, such as a villain or dragon popping in. However, I don't think it's really necessary for you to afford your clients quite the same level of protection – no, grab it for yourself. (If your clients are subsequently attacked by a fire-breathing dragon, I will refund the cost of this book.)

All of this preparation surrounding where you should sit should take only a few seconds. There will be a temptation to stand there for half an hour, deep in thought, figuring out your optimum seating position. Just go for one of the above rules and grab your seat.

You see, musical chairs, while being an entertaining diversion for you as a child, was in fact intensive training to prepare you for this moment.

By the way, a late arrival, as detailed above, would also leave you with no choice of seat. You may have to sit, zombified, under a lighthouse beacon of energy, backlit by what could only be described as a nuclear explosion of white light, at the mercy of any invader.

ARE YOU IN OR OUT?

The way you sit in a meeting reveals a great deal about you. You may notice how very senior people often sit the same way. They tend to recline into their seat as if very comfortable – without a worry in the world. In this most laid-back of positions, they will often put their hands behind their heads as if they were on some sunny beach relaxing in the sunshine.

What is happening here is an open display of perceived power, showing clear disrespect to juniors and at the same time telegraphing their fixed seniority. With this pose, they are saying *"Hey, I'm so important that I no longer have to make any effort. I am top of this tree. I don't have to care about you lot. You better prove yourself worthy or you're fired. Yeah, that's it ... you're all FIRED!"*

The worst thing is that we let them get away with it. "Sit forwards!" I want to shout at these people ... but I never do.

It is therefore important that you constantly look at your own "seated display" and check that it is always communicating positive thoughts and ideas about who you are and what you represent.

Imagine an invisible curtain of air between the edge of the table and the ceiling. Your job is to ensure that your face is sticking through this curtain of air and placing you IN the meeting. If you are sitting back, you are electing to be OUT of the meeting. You need to be in.

To do this even more effectively, don't allow your back to touch the back of the chair. You should push the chair slightly back, perch on its front edge and lean into the meeting – lean into your future.

WHO ARE YOU AGAIN?

People love their names to be known, remembered and announced publicly, so addressing people by name when you speak is a great way of delivering on that need.

But many of us can have a problem remembering names and faces, and your big-opportunity meeting can be made even more nerve-wracking if you're presented with a whole array of new people to meet. It might be possible to be sent beforehand a list of the people who will be attending the meeting – ask your client's PA – so that at least you can familiarize yourself with the names and job titles. But if that's not possible, here's a subtle way for you to solve any attack of "namenesia" that you may suffer in a meeting featuring new people.

At the beginning of the session, when people typically hand out business cards to each other, take careful note of who people are and where they are sitting. Carefully set out the cards that you have been given in a semicircle in front of you with each card's table position corresponding to where that person is seated. So, if Jason is to the right of Melissa who in turn is to the right of Jeff, lay out their cards in that order. In this way, as long as you have done it right (!), all you need to do is glance down to see the name of the person who is speaking.

If there are no cards flying around, create a little written display of names on the top of your notepaper with each name corresponding to where that person is sitting around the table. You just have to hope that they don't all suddenly head off to the bathroom and return to completely different seats!

Warning: Name checking is a gamble. As much as people love their name to be remembered and mentioned publicly, they hate it when their name has been forgotten, then incorrectly offered up in front of others. Sometimes people become too shy and uncomfortable to point out the error. Let me take another episode of *Seinfeld* as an example. The key character Elaine is wrongly called "Susie" by one of her office colleagues. Elaine never corrects the error, but instead descends into a catalogue of lies in order to protect her good name. There then ensues hilarious scenes as the boss demands to see both Elaine AND Susie ... So, when it comes to someone's name:

**IF YOU'RE
NOT SURE,
SAY NO MORE!**

WAIT FOR IT ...!

Management guru Peter Drucker said it: "Listen first, speak last." Even though you will be absolutely loaded with fascinating things to say and content to contribute to this meeting, sometimes – in fact most of the time – it truly pays to wait.

When booking me, many of my clients make the same request. They say, "*When you coach the team, can you make sure that they are listening as well – no one listens to each other in this company.*"

READY, SET, *LISTEN*

In any meeting situation, first take in all the data, messages (verbal and non verbal) and crucial information. Only *then*, from that newly informed position, state your case. You will automatically be more prepared, more relevant and more effective.

WHAT'S *REALLY* BEING SAID

Listening to someone's words is often an exercise in being able to translate what is *really* being said. Being able to read between the lines is a valuable skill in your continuous flow of communication soft skills. Let's have a look at some examples:

That office needs a good cleaning.
Clean that office. It's a bloody mess!

I wonder what the traffic will be like later.
Please let me go early.

… and we could also try a different approach.
This doesn't work. It needs changing.

I like it. How about we also try it without the music?
I hate the music. It won't work.

I think I may be dying.
I don't feel well.

Not bad. Do you think it'll work?
It's bad. Seriously, this won't work.

Whether it's tact, fear, politeness or just avoidance, people will often skirt around what they truly want to say and introduce confused comments that don't help anyone! My military clients never do this. They learn pretty early on that, in the battlefield, if you issue a command such as:

"Not sure, but we might think about launching a three-way attack on the enemy quite soon – but then again we might not."

... no one will be safe. In the armed forces, absolute clarity of instruction and order of command give all soldiers clear and unambiguous confidence in what to do and when to do it.

In the rest of the world, this sort of clarity is sadly lacking, and we need to translate what we think is being said, rather than take the words at face value.

Obviously, you need to be constantly aware that what is being said to you might not actually be what is truly meant or felt. Most people understand this, but few deal well with overtly conflicting messages – leaving people desperate to shout, "*Just say it!*"

TAKING NOTES

People want to feel as if their words matter. They want to be assured that their ideas and contributions really count for something. If they are clients or bosses, they want to know that their instructions and guidance will be followed. One of the easiest ways that you can demonstrate that you are really listening in a meeting is to make handwritten notes as the person in front of you is speaking.

Theoretically, of course, if you are sitting at a distance, you could be writing anything at all, and still win points simply for the act of writing. He could be blabbing on about infrastructure security issues and you could be writing *"Must buy a cat,"* but it looks like you are fully immersed in his ideas – so much so that you feel forced to write them down!

Is it acceptable to take notes on a laptop? There are pros and cons, and people continue to debate the issue:

PROS
- You appear up to date with technology.
- Typing is a whole lot faster than handwriting.
- You can easily file, sort and keep the notes you take for better future use.

CONS

- The raised lid of a laptop forms a barrier between you and the client.
- The laptop can place you OUT of the meeting (see pages 117–8), as you are busy looking at your screen rather than making eye contact with the people around you.
- You can become so engrossed in your note-taking that you forget to contribute to the meeting.
- You can easily forget to save a file and lose everything.
- It might appear that you are just catching up on your email, playing a game or answering IMs from "hotplayer703".

Regarding laptop use … I'm going to allow it, but with some disclaimers. Note-taking on a laptop is probably better kept for those larger meetings attended by quite a lot of people seated around a large table. That way the "barrier" effect is reduced. In a smaller, more informal meeting, it can look like overkill, so here you're probably better with just pen and paper. Use your judgement and assess the individual situation. If other people get their laptops out, then that's obviously an encouraging sign for you to do the same.

You can protect yourself and enhance your overall impact by making an announcement as you start up your slim wi-fi-enabled Notebook, PC or iBook. Simply state *"Let me take some notes here"*, then start tapping away furiously, even though you are just typing *"Thursday meeting about things"*.

THE LIGHTHOUSE OF EYE CONTACT

Whether you are in control of the meeting or not, whether you are "selling" or "buying", performing or observing, what you choose to do with your eyes in a meeting can affect your level of success. There are many people who retreat into their personal safety zone by lowering their eyes and, in effect, withdrawing from the meeting. Eye contact is a crucial element of all human interaction, but it must be measured, appropriate and delivered to the right people at the right time to really maximize its effect. When you connect with someone's eyes during a meeting, a number of things are going on:

1   You are establishing a temporary bond, something that pays off as the meeting goes on. Once established, you can repeat the glance checking for reaction, response, visual opinion and interest. This can be very useful in establishing a start to a new business relationship. After "eye-connecting" several times with someone during a meeting, you are within your soft-skills rights to go up to them after it's all done, ask their opinion and lay down an anchor point which you can use later on to reconnect. If you have made absolutely no eye contact with someone, it is harder to then approach them afterwards.

2   You are including people in what is going on. It is all too easy for people to feel excluded from a meeting that features dull or irrelevant content. To ensure that those people feel included and part of the session, you should endeavour to make eye contact with them as often as possible. This makes them feel that at least *you* think that they should be part of this and that it would be plain rude to behave otherwise!

3   You keep people awake. There is the temptation, if you are not a star player in a meeting, to simply drift off into a state of "boardroom sleep". This is characterized, at best, by continuously staring out of the window or at the cookies on the table and, at worst, by actually falling asleep and slumping downwards. When people know that your "lighthouse" of eye contact will keep consistently swinging around and illuminating them, they will feel the need to remain alert and part of the meeting.

WHERE TO LOOK

We have established that we should be making eye contact with people – but which people? Sometimes, in meetings with new clients, there are a lot of people present. Where and when should we concentrate our eye-contact activity?

The answer has to be: everyone, always.

A client of mine told me a story about how they had developed a new video game for one of the major game-playing consoles (no more details – must protect the innocent … and guilty!) The day arrived for the big pitch meeting, and my client had arranged for three key players to meet with the potential buying firm. Opposite our three heroes sat eight people from the games company.

There was the big boss, several intellectual-property lawyers, a couple of major honchos and a "bunch of nobodies" – at least, that's how the setup was described to me. As the meeting went on, our three heroes directed all their effort, performance and delivery to the big boss. After all, he was the holder of the purse strings and would make the ultimate decision.

He did not, however, act alone. Those "nobodies" were there to observe for a reason. After the meeting, by all accounts, the big boss turned to these extra players and asked what they had thought – whether this new games company could become a partner or not. The "nobodies" (who were actually "somebodies") revealed their displeasure. Nobody from our heroes' team had even looked at them. They hadn't felt included and this rankled with them. As a result, our three heroes didn't win the job.

It is crucially important to remember that *everyone* in that meeting can affect the outcome of your success. Make sure that they are all part of what you do and say – no matter how junior they may appear.

OBSERVE AND REACT

Once the time comes for you to respond and make your contribution, constantly monitor the reaction your comments and ideas receive. Obviously you are hoping to see nods and smiles, but if you read a general lack of interest or no clear buy-in – in other words, you aren't getting a good NPM (nods-per-minute rate) – follow up your now rather feeble sounding initial plan with some disclaimer like, "*That's one idea, but obviously there are other directions that we could also explore …*"

If, on the other hand, everyone is nodding, smiling and buying into your plan, suddenly there can arise the temptation to add more, to conjure additional ideas … to go overboard and to oversell.

Don't do it. Keep quiet. Enough already!

You have had your moment and if, like a comedian trying to better the best laugh of the night, you push on and fail, you might actually undo all of the great impact you have just created.

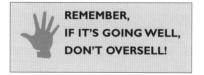

**REMEMBER,
IF IT'S GOING WELL,
DON'T OVERSELL!**

Your job is done. That promotion is coming. Enjoy the glow.

THE DOCTOR, THE ANALYST AND THE LAWYER

No, not a weak joke. Rather, I want to encourage you to *think* like a doctor, *research* like an analyst, and *deliver* like a lawyer.

Your performance in the boardroom is something that can really open up big opportunities. People need to trust in all aspects of you. How you look, speak and deliver all contribute to your final effectiveness score (see pages 15–16). So how can you improve the game you choose to play?

I like to encourage my clients to up their game by imagining themselves in certain roles as they build up to an appearance of some sort. The inspiring roles of doctor, analyst and lawyer are a good start.

If you are to make an impression in a meeting with clients or bosses, you need to tell them something that they don't know. You must first diagnose the problem like a medical practitioner; next back up your opinion with solid research of the industry, competitors and the market place; and finally deliver your findings in a confident and informed manner. You should try to use messaging that encompasses and deals with negative comments that critics might use, along with your positive ideas and concepts.

Let's imagine you are part of a marketing meeting aimed at planning future strategy in the airline industry.

THE DOCTOR DIAGNOSES THE PROBLEM

Airlines have been suffering from bad publicity about delays, poor re-booking policy and overcrowding.

THE ANALYST RESEARCHES THE CAUSE

People are vociferous when things go wrong and often go straight to the media. In fact, in 2007 during the great snowstorms in the United States,

39 per cent more people than ever before aired their personal complaints in the media and on-line. This statistic is hard to argue against. A well-researched fact such as this is far more impressive than a vague statement such as: "*I'm sure more people complain in the winter.*"

THE LAWYER ARGUES THE CASE

As a possible solution, you conclude that there is a need to look at finding positive, feel-good stories during the easy times – when the airlines actually deliver on their promises. You say, "*If all the public are currently seeing is the bad news, we need to deliver the good. Let's put out a search for the best flying experience, with prizes on offer for the passengers and airlines.*"

A great lawyer will air his opponent's views before that opponent has a chance to do so himself, and will then immediately defeat them with solid arguments. You should do the same – take the wind out of their sails and leave them with nowhere else to go.

Back to our example. In this case, a naysayer might be expected to pipe up with the observation, "*Good news doesn't make the news.*" Having anticipated this, you will already have said, "*Now, many people will say that good news doesn't sell well and that is usually true, so we spin this as bad news for the train and car-hire companies. Bad news for Hertz and Amtrak as airlines start making customers happy again.*"

Using this method you have destroyed your opponents argument before they have even made it. This method is known as "self-debate".

POSITIVE SANDWICH

In other instances, you'll still get a mixed response to your proposal, and the client or colleague will probably want to chip in with their own comments and ideas. The difficulty arises when the client's ideas are not very good! Here is a soft-skills approach to handling the ideas of others. The positive sandwich is pretty simple. You just sandwich your guidance and comments between two positive observations.

Imagine you are a party planner dealing with a client who has ideas of their own.

Creative client: *"Given that the theme is 'tropical island paradise' can we have, like, a little pile of sand on the centre of each table?"*

You (knowing this won't work!): *"Ooh, like a little beach – I love that idea. Actually, what might be even better – and easier for the serving staff – is if we create a bigger beach at the entrance to the room, put coconuts on it; we can bring in some real palms, and on the tables we could have more palm fronds and shells, which will look great. But what a good thought about the sand."*

What you have neatly done here is deliver a positive sandwich. You have said that you love the idea and that you believe that this was a good thought, yet, in between this positivity, you have gently redirected the client to doing it your (better) way.

Now, it's more than possible that the client will stand their ground and demand sand all over the place and you will, naturally, comply with their wishes. Dealing with their ideas in a positive and inspiring fashion, however, makes everyone feel good and will help you to keep more control as the planning continues.

OFFERING CHOICES

This is actually a good way to keep control. Giving people options is a smart way to make *them* feel in control, while still retaining for yourself a win-win outcome.

In his book *Billion Dollar Kiss* – about the US TV industry – Jeffrey Stepakoff reveals that a TV executive would much rather buy a one-paragraph idea about a new TV show than a fully worked, finished and "ready-to-shoot" 100-page script.

The reason, Stepakoff claims, is that the TV executive wants to feel that he, in some way, helped to develop and control the project. Simply buying a completed script would not endear him to his bosses and would prevent him from proving his worth as a TV developer.

Similarly, when we present ideas to people, handing them control by offering them options centred on your concept allows them to feel a little more powerful – as if they have made a choice, a decision. They don't want to feel pinned into a corner. And, offering an all-or-nothing single-option proposal greatly raises the stakes for you, too. You've just left yourself with a 50:50 outcome: Yes, or No. Once they've already said No, it's far harder to get them to reconsider, or present them with other options. Far better to present them with several options in the first place; that way they are far more likely to go with at least one of them.

Naturally, in making this work for you, the trick is to offer choices that *all* suit you down to the ground, so it doesn't really matter which one they pick, as long as they pick one. (Think Henry Ford and the colour black!) Let's look at some examples:

You: *"We've put together a fabulous $100,000 event that will win you loads of PR and really put you on the map, this is what we recommend."*

Your client: *"Hmmm, we were thinking of something different, but thanks for coming in."*

You: *"You could spend $10,000 on a smaller more exclusive and classy event, $50,000 on an impressive party and launch that will have people talking or, if you like, we've put together some ideas on an amazing $100,000 evening that would truly grab headlines and win a lot of PR.*

Your client: *"We were thinking about the smaller more chic event, so let's talk about that one......"*

You are covering your bases here and giving them a full range of choices – and they are going to need one. There are no guarantees, but at least you won't be thrown out because their favoured option wasn't included.

MAKE INTELLIGENT MISTAKES

When dealing with a boss – as opposed to a client, you may sometimes need to deliver something different – not choices, but deliberate mistakes.

A very talented TV producer in the United Kingdom, Ben Frow, who has held senior creative positions at several major networks, reached these heights of success through being both gifted and diplomatic. In his younger days, when he was busy producing video "lifestyle features", he would deliberately include a couple of shots that weren't quite good enough. He knew it and, more importantly, he knew that his boss would instantly spot them.

Why would he deliberately allow himself to be corrected during the review process? Why would he reveal himself to have made some odd judgement calls?

What Ben was doing was acknowledging that his boss, in a predictably consistent effort to justify his senior position, would make changes, regardless of how good the edited item was. This man was going to pick Ben up on something, and probably end up ruining a perfectly good item. So Ben chose to offer up the bait of a couple of shots that he was happy to lose. This way, his final "edit" would still look great *and* his boss would feel as if he had served his purpose and could go off and have cocktails.

Ben had observed that his boss had this need to do *something,* so he gave him something to do, while still retaining control. He observed, he listened and he responded; he took advantage of the situation – great soft skills!

ULTRA-NEGATIVITY

If you wish to deliver a very negative message within a meeting, all you have to do is combine the lean-back motion with the crossing of the arms (see pages 115–16). If you want your visual NO to be really emphatic, you could lean back and examine your fingernails instead. Either way, this body language has a very dark cloud surrounding it. If you see or deliver this action, it means that things are very bad. It is the visual equivalent of saying any or all of the following messages:

"Uchhh, I hate this idea. I hate you. I hate this job. I don't want to be here, and I simply won't play!"

Unless you truly want to transmit this message – you should never do it! If you see it happening in front of you, however, you may want to change tactics, alter your approach and try to identify what turned them off.

THE BOARDROOM BRIBE

Some time ago, I was invited to meet the staff of a leading-speaker agency in London. They regularly held a lunchtime session where, as a group, after their internal meeting, they would invite in new speakers, listen to what they had to say, then decide whether to sign them up or not. The approach was an effective one, and they had been doing it for a while.

I decided that, if I were to stand out, I not only had to impress with my content and delivery, but I also needed to bring along something that would create an additional "memory anchor". Just before the meeting, I went into Selfridges on Oxford Street and purchased the largest container of Jelly Bellies I could find.

As I'm sure you know, these are the tiny multiflavoured candies that can become very addictive. Were they right for a meeting with people in the "event" industry? Well, they have a fun but not childlike image, and I wanted something that would be memorable and appropriate – not over the top, but something a bit above the ordinary. Jelly Bellies it was!

I entered the meeting – very much a pitch scenario – and began by saying, *"I want to start this relationship with you in the way I mean to go on* [reaching for gift now] *with a clear and obvious bribe so that you will like me."*

I placed the Jelly Bellies on the table and there was an instant and positive reaction (phew!). There was a good laugh and much excitement as the container was passed around. By using a bit of reverse psychology, stating the obvious and employing a touch of self-deprecation, I was able to win over this young yet professional group.

For the next month, in email exchanges between myself and the individual agents who had attended that meeting, they constantly referred to how popular the candies had proven and how that, now they were all consumed, I may have to come back.

HOW TO DEAL WITH ABSOLUTE POWER

As we move up through our careers, we more frequently come across people who possess real power. They may not control arsenals of weaponry, but they do have the authority to action decisions that would have a material effect on you one way or another.

Naturally these powerful decision-makers never sign deals, promote you or approve mergers for *your* benefit. No, it will always be for the benefit of their company, their shareholders or simply themselves. Be under no illusion: this is not charity. Their decisions are going to be based on making their own lives easier (promoting someone who can take on more responsibility) or their business more profitable (accepting a great pitch).

The reason I remind you of this apparently obvious fact is that so may many people trudge through life moaning that they "deserved" the pay rise or promotion that they never received, that they should have won that pitch on which they had spent so much time.

This thinking is entirely wrong. What they should be saying is *"I failed to make him see how crucial I would have been for his organization's success."* It is a subtle alteration in thinking, but it is this slight mind-set difference that will help you to influence and win over other people. The former mind-set traps you into being a powerless victim, at the mercy of the whims of an all-powerful decision-maker. The latter puts the ball back in your court, gives you the initiative and encourages you to look for different approaches and techniques to achieve what you want.

One of the best examples of this "absolute power" is the wholly arbitrary decision-making exercised by top TV executives who appoint (I could say "anoint" here!) unknowns to top TV shows instantly turning these – often hapless – people into stars. This overwhelming power to turn a nobody into a millionaire, almost overnight confers an almost demigod-like status on the TV executives in command.

These top executives will never pick someone because they feel that this specific person deserves a chance. No, they see their selection and promotion of these people as a way of climbing further up their own ladder of success. If you are a TV producer and you pick someone who goes on to be a rating-winning megastar, you will always be the one who discovered him/her. You will ride their wave to the top as the brilliant mind behind the major celebrity. This is why some utterly unthinkable, dreadful TV "personalities" are never taken off the air. This is simply because the aforementioned TV producer would, in this instance, be admitting some sort of critical failure, an admission of having got it wrong. And, guess what … they don't like doing that very often.

So, when faced with a powerful player, your entire thinking must shift. You must become the key to their success. You must talk and act in a way that fills the player with confidence about you as a trusted adviser dedicated and contributing to their success.

The other chameleon-like change is the need to create that fake-friendship bond. In other words, people like people who are similar to themselves (review chapter 4, where we have already learned how to establish commonality with your "targets"). If you go into a meeting with your boss or prospective client all quiet, subservient and humble, they will see you as simply what you are – just one of the team, a drone bee or worker ant, beavering away and not deserving any distinction above the others. You have not positioned yourself as a thinker, as a leader or as an adviser. As a result you won't be seen as one.

You need to change your approach – add something to the mix that gets you noticed and respected. I want that player to look at you, consider what you just blurted out and say, *"Hey, that's a good idea! Who are you again?"*

There is, of course, a risk here that sticking your head above the parapet and effectively shouting, *"Look at me. That's right, I have some pretty good ideas!"* might well result in you being knocked back and stared at by everyone else in the meeting, in a horrible moment of embarrassed silence tinged with pity. But, if you don't take risks – you'll never get picked.

Let's just take this moment one step further. Here's the scenario: you are sitting round the table in the boardroom with a group of people. There are you and several others at a similar level to you, then there's the big boss or important client.

You have a solid, well-planned idea, and you are ready to deliver. Picking your time is crucial, as is the language that you choose to use. At this momentous point, it is very important that you position what you are about to say as a suggestion, something to be considered, not a *fait accompli*. You are not about to wager your entire career and everything you have worked towards on the outcome of this moment, nor should you present it as a "my-way-or-the-highway" solution.

Instead, in a calm and measured voice, and at an appropriate moment, you say, *"Now, this may not be the optimal approach, but I have a feeling that if we use a tagline such as 'No More Surprises' we could encapsulate all of our USPs* (unique selling points) *in a single thought. I'm sure this can be improved upon, but it might be a good start."*

Key phrases within this fictitious statement are *"may not be ... optimal"*, *"could encapsulate"* and *"might be a good start"*. With all of these phrases, you have let yourself off the hook if the assembled team think that your idea is utter tripe. If they love it, however, they will jump on it and use the keys that you offered to build upon it. But that initial idea is yours. You shone, and everyone knows it.

When YOU Are The Boss

They say that the only thing that is harder than getting to the top is staying there. How can you use a variety of soft skills to ensure that you do indeed stay at the top of your game?

STAFF MANAGEMENT

Among many other things, great leadership involves getting the best out of (and encouraging) others' frantic activity while taking a step back to consider the bigger picture. According to Tim Sanders, the author of *The Likeability Factor, "people don't quit bad jobs, they quit bad bosses"*. It is more important than ever that you are perceived among your team to be a worthwhile leader, someone they respect, admire and can look up to. Although this book is not a leadership manual per se, your role as the leader in the boardroom or of a team is worthy of examination.

As a leader or boss, your job has many facets: to motivate, direct, encourage and inspire. You must create value, add experience and, of course, earn your money in your own right. Everyone has their particular managerial style, but, undoubtedly, those bosses who are liked and respected by their teams usually do well. Loyalty, productivity and high employee satisfaction all go hand in hand with a good senior–junior relationship.

Don't become conceited like those TV stars I've already mentioned and imagine that your success is purely down to your personal brilliance! No doubt that success is also due, in part, to a bit of good luck and to the cumulative contribution made by a whole team of people operating beneath you, almost without you noticing it.

One of the key measures of you as a leader is how good you are at retaining great people beneath you. The more stars you see walking out the door, the more you need to polish up your communication skills and find ways to personally and professionally reconnect with that potential body of exodus staff – *before* they reach the door.

At a recent event I attended in Washington, DC, the subject of "resourcing" – the ability to deploy the right people to the right job at the right time – arose.

This particular firm was enjoying growth and profitability, but was running up against problems in hiring the right people and retaining the right teams. In a booming market, everyone wants to grow, and demands for people resources meant that this firm's plans might be curtailed.

The new head of HR (which someone light-heartedly informed me stood for "Human Remains") made an excellent point about the different measures that senior partners could take in order to retain their people, while not costing the firm any extra money. She mentioned that the results of a recent survey showed that employees valued "recognition" as much as pay. Public recognition rather than a private email was, it turned out, a major motivator in keeping people in position and working hard. We all still like a pat on the back, a "Well done", especially if it is seen by everyone.

Around the boardroom table, you can apply this same approach.

HANDING OUT CREDIT

Do you remember the last time someone credited you with having a winning idea or hailing the success of something you had just achieved? Whether it was simply people round the dinner table thanking you for making such a fabulous meal or the chairman of the board singling you out as being responsible for a huge upswing in profitability – it all feels good.

If you deconstruct what's going on, you'll discover that it is all about advertising. Someone takes it upon themselves to advertise the fact that you are great. They put this idea into the minds of all of those listening and watching. People who are already your friends and those whom you seek to impress will all receive this message at the same time. You are worth doing business with.

It doesn't take much persuasion for you to realize the value – how good it feels – of that little bit of public recognition. Now that you realize the power a bit of "public credit payout" can bring, it's time to start handing it out to others. One of the best places to do this is in the boardroom.

Why bother? Well, if you make others feel good about something they have done, they are far more likely to listen to you and your ideas. They will respect you more. They will feel indebted to you for what you have said (payback credit!), and you may just find it that much easier to retain the talent you have nurtured.

"Joe's execution on that travel company IPO was fabulous. How about building on that success [gesturing at Joe, while glancing around the entire table] by contacting every other unlisted travel company and inviting them in for a luxury breakfast and presentation on how we did it. By convincing them we have something of value to hand over, we should tempt them to come in, we'll make new contacts and we would probably win new business"

This is clearly your idea – after all, you are the boss! Yet, with diplomacy and maturity, you make it sound as if you are simply building on Joe's brilliance. Joe doesn't feel threatened – quite the opposite, he's flattered at you drawing attention to his hard work. He's been given his due credit. The rest of the team already know of Joe's work and are likewise impressed that you have credited him. They can see that you have not just generated a new idea, but have, once again, justified your leadership. More than this, Joe's colleagues now also want similar recognition, and will work that much harder to attract your attention to their ideas and enterprises.

Handing out credit is a simple gesture and works well.

FREE PARKING

One IT firm that I work with in Fairfax, Virginia, handles one aspect of giving out this recognition in a novel and effective fashion. They reserve one parking space, closest to the front door of the company's HQ, for "this month's star" with that employee's name proudly printed on the golden plaque.

The parking spot is much coveted and, when the employee in question receives the award, not only does he or she get a fabulous parking spot for four weeks, but everyone else sees it every day on their way into the office.

That's a double win. The only downside is that, when your month is completed, you are sent back to Row ZZ 9!

UNEXPECTED GENEROSITY

The theory of payback (see pages 16–17) works for you as a boss just as much as in any other position. As a leader, however you have the chance to occasionally surprise your team with an unexpected gift or gesture that leaves them with their morale boosted – *and* feeling as if they owe you.

The annual Christmas party does not qualify as unexpected and doesn't in itself create additional goodwill among your people. Here are a few examples of the kind of gesture that might, in the medium term, boost goodwill and productivity, as well as increase staff morale, loyalty and commitment.

- Give your employees Friday afternoon off for no reason – let them go and enjoy the weekend!

- Invite in a lunchtime speaker to tell a few amusing and practical anecdotes, introducing fresh concepts in a relaxed manner while simultaneously showing how much you value your people.

- Bring in a big box of good-quality candy or chocolates for your team.

In fact, I know a large and very successful law firm in London that ensures that there are fabulous fresh chocolate brownies at every meeting –

whether internal or external, or both. This little bonus has absolutely no effect on the law nor this particular firm's method of practising it. Every one of their clients now knows about the brownies, however, they look forward to them and have become a talking point. Here we see a working example of how spending $15 can create a warm, memorable and compelling link between staff, bosses, clients and lawyers.

SET AN AGENDA – THEN STICK TO IT!

The one thing more valuable than chocolate and candy is time – other people's time. As an effective, inspirational and popular leader, it is your job to show how much you value other people and their time. One great way to do this is to hand them the "gift of time".

The opposite of this gift is what most of us experience almost on a daily basis. This is where you turn up at a meeting at 10am which is scheduled to end at 11am. What could be simpler than that? But it doesn't quite work out that way.

Instead, at 11.20am, as the meeting trundles on into the darkest recesses of boredom and irrelevance, attendees start to realize that the published schedule, agenda and intended duration were all lies – a joke not a business tool – and that this meeting has become a forum for show-off dictator wannabes and attention-grabbing halfwits. Time is lost for ever, attention wanes and everyone silently decides that, once again, they need to polish up their résumé.

To win your team over and give them something that will enhance their loyalty and build their enthusiasm, you will now not only make sure that you run that meeting to time, keeping a check on those who wish to dominate and control, but also go one step further.

From now on, you will send out those email meeting invitations and indicate that the meeting is scheduled to take two hours – a far more generous estimate of what you know you will need. Once in the meeting, however, you ensure that all essential business is taken care of within just 90 minutes.

At this point you give the gift of time. You proudly announce, just like those airline captains who arrive at the destination gate early, that you are ahead of time, everything has been completed and that they all are free to go. Like a generous jailer, you free your prisoners way ahead of their parole date – this is the "gift of time".

People are stunned, they quizzically look at their watches and each other, and wonder what on earth is going on. And they decide that you are the *best* boss ... ever, and this was the finest meeting ever!

Don't forget meetings and the boardroom are just one part of the mix. Your job, as you continue to strategically communicate and deploy your fabulous soft skills is to make other people feel good about their interaction with you. It is also to ensure that you are saying what people want to hear and doing what they want to see. Your ultimate objective is, of course, your success – but your actions should continually seem focused on your targets.

CHAPTER 7

Techniquette –
the Etiquette of Technology

> For a long time I resisted bringing this kind of thing up at my events and seminars, as it felt almost like instructing people who had never been to an office before on how to behave. But, as the months rolled on, more and more people would complain about how badly their colleagues, friends and partners acted around gadgets.

BlackBerries, smartphones, PDAs, cell phones, sidekicks, pagers, iPhones – it didn't matter what the gadget was, the reaction around them was consistent: people didn't like what they were seeing.

We all have our favourite device, whether it's the smartphone, BlackBerry, iPhone, Palm Centro, Palm Treo or Motorola Q, and we clutch them like actual cash – constantly glancing at their screens, their flashing lights, their indicators of how much others need us.

Now it's important to say that I have a serious affection (bordering on obsession!) for gadgets of all kinds – cameras, cell phones, portable DVD players, personal video recorders, laptops, printers, scanners, laser mice – the lot. So I am certainly not some crazed Luddite imploring you to run outside and burn all of your electronic devices while dancing around screaming. I do advocate that they should be used frequently – but considerately.

GADGET POKER

Let's face it, it is predominantly men who enjoy showing off the latest flashing, buzzing, touch-sensitive little devices, and the way that we tend to do it is to play what I call "gadget poker".

Picture the scene: two guys in their thirties sitting opposite each other at lunch. In a similar method to revealing your final hand in poker, they start to deal out each of their individual gadgets. It's all done in a very nonchalant manner but, as each gadget is laid down on the lunch table between the two players, it's very clear that the gentlemen in question are vying for the title of top gadget king.

First out – a Motorola Razr. Hmmm, not bad, but a little bit 2005, I'm sure you'll agree. Now the game is on, and the second guy produces a Motorola Krazr. That's definitely a better device, so our second guy is in the lead in this round of gadget poker – but, hold on, what's this?

Our first guy produces a Palm Treo – fancy! Not to be outdone, our second player proudly lays down a Sony Reader (with 1000 books downloaded into its memory!). An impressive hand so far, but the book reader could be a little frivolous. Hang on … this could be the winner – our first contestant produces a flashing BlackBerry Curve replete with 10 unread messages, and secures the winning hand! Hooray! (Okay, I accept the iPhone could also win that hand … but I still love BlackBerry!)

Now this style of one-upmanship in terms of gadget pride can actually produce a great bond between two people whose shared interest is the ever changing world of electronic gadgetry. However, the great risk when laying out your gadgets at a meeting or lunch table – when hopefully there are fantastic deals to be clinched – is that you will be very tempted to look at them. Distracting, and not good etiquette.

If you really want to win at gadget poker, however, you can use it to establish trust (see pages 76–87) with a new contact or client. You should make out that one of your client's devices is actually the one that you have always lusted after. For example, if you put down your BlackBerry, you should show extreme interest in his Treo. Your expression of enthusiasm makes your target feel good about their choice, and positions you as someone who makes them feel comfortable and perhaps even special.

I LOVE YOU

Now I *know* what it feels like when my BlackBerry receives a message – that gentle tone and pulsing light combine to let me know that I have friends, that people need me, that my services are required! It's like a mesmerizing siren on the shores of some tropical island drawing me in … occupying my mind … and my soul! Who can resist this unique and powerful call? That device is telling me that I am *loved*!

Imagine you are sitting at a lunch with a client or colleague, or even your boss, and your BlackBerry or other messaging device suddenly sparks into life. It would take great power, poise and control for you not to look at that flashing screen. The vast majority of us would glance briefly or indeed for a while longer at the information therein.

But be warned. When you do this, you are saying to the person sitting directly in front of you: *"At this moment, whatever is on my screen is now more important than you."* If you are happy to convey that message to the person with you then, by all means, go ahead and consult your device.

However, I would suggest that, in order to take advantage of the effect that soft skills can have on other people, you should take your BlackBerry or cell phone at the beginning of the session, and deliberately and openly place it into your bag to show your companions that, for the duration of the meeting, they are now your number one focus.

BLUETOOTH

Bluetooth earpieces are a fabulous piece of technology. Great for when you are rushing around with bags or sitting in traffic, your Bluetooth earpiece gives you the freedom to continue doing business and stay in touch. What I've started to see on a frighteningly large number of occasions, however, is that some people (always men for some reason) elect to keep that earpiece in their ears during meetings and other face-to-face communication.

Unless you are from *Star Trek*'s Borg Collective or this device has been surgically grafted into your skull, it *must* be removed before you talk to another human being. There's nothing else to say.

INSTANT MESSAGING (IM)

Instant messaging is becoming more and more of an accepted method of fast communication. Within companies, it is an efficient way of quickly posing questions, getting instant responses and keeping things casual. Nice.

But you should still apply certain rules. IM can keep a record of your chats, as long as you select the appropriate option; it can then find that bizarrely named file in your system for you.

This is not a reliable way of keeping track of key decisions and opinions. It is my belief that, if you are approaching something of real value with a client, friend or colleague, you should switch to email so that you can accurately record and keep the comments committed to a searchable, printable, quotable digital file.

As you progress further into IM, the temptation to conduct communication like a 15-year-old text-messaging addict will become overwhelming. *"LOL BOS BRB"* might well end up being your way of saying, *"Laugh out loud. Boss looking over shoulder. I'll be right back."*

With the closest of friends this is acceptable; with everyone else, you are voluntarily altering your on-line image and reinventing yourself as a sulking teenager. Your call.

CORPORATE DATABOMBS

If you really want to infuriate somebody, send them a "corporate databomb". This is when you send a stream of photos, graphics, giant PowerPoint file or video that you either couldn't be bothered or didn't know how to compress for email. As a result, it's a weighty file consuming 20MB of space, which screws up inboxes, fires off a bunch of Mailer-Daemon (what *is* that?) error messages and creates inconvenience and long download times.

Show good techniquette when sending email attachments, and always find a way to compress large files before sending them. (The same goes for PowerPoint presentations. Simply find any image in the presentation, right click on format and select compress. When the software asks if you would like to compress all images in the file, you click, *"Hell, yes!"* Now that's a good e-citizen!)

EMAIL ETIQUETTE

Not sure how old you are but, if you're more than 30 years old, it's most likely that you were never taught about email at school. No one ever sat you down, banged on the board at the front of the room and scribbled *"EMAIL!"*

No one went through any rules, as those rules simply didn't exist. And they don't really exist now. Who is to say what is right and what is wrong about the way we send and deal with email? It's just there – and it's fabulous, right? I love it. Email is fast, effective and allows me to stay in the loop wherever I am, whatever I am doing.

Email feeds us information, news, gossip, business, connections, opportunities and, of course, a daily chance to help an ex-Nigerian minister give you millions of dollars. (Can you believe that people actually fall for that scam?)

Not surprisingly, there are always a few Luddites who proudly trumpet that they don't reply to email or that they'll deal with it in their own sweet time, or even that it's ruining old-fashioned business values. Sure, like the telephone ruined the good old-fashioned telegraph service, or the railroads ruined the great Pony Express opportunity!

For those of us who desire success and who are fully in charge of our destinies – ignoring email is ignoring business. You might as well hang up on your clients in the middle of phone calls, or leave halfway through a job and still expect to be paid. Email is not going away; it is here to stay, and its use is only going to become even more widespread. It will evolve, but this real-time, live and ultra-fast communication is our new norm. We demand nothing less.

Not only that, but your ever-growing database of email has great worth as well. It is the most valuable, searchable data. The newest versions of operating systems are finally offering a spectacular instantaneous search facility, giving you total power, knowledge and absolute control over everything you have ever sent or received.

Email should be encouraged and driven hard in order to build that mine of data faster than ever before – it is one of your prime assets. To be an effective soft-skills communicator, you must ensure that people welcome your emails. They must react to your name in their inbox by opening your mail with enthusiasm, not by dreading, deleting, junking or ignoring it. The recipients of your email should anticipate something relevant, brief, interesting, new, appropriate and of value. If your message isn't checking at least some of these boxes, you may want to rethink sending it at all.

There are several key rules that should govern the way you email from now on.

SPELLING AND GRAMMAR

Above all, the most important rule is that you must respect spelling and grammar. Who decided that, just because the message is electronic in form, we can totally dismiss checking it through for typos, grammatical errors and horrors of punctuation? Sure, email is fast, but that doesn't mean you're in some frenzied keyboard race where all that matters is dispatching a stream of half-words in an attempt to become the world's fastest typist.

When you send a message, you are sending a bit of you – you are saying *"Hey, check this out … After years of education, experience and wisdom, this is how I write!"* How do you want people to see you? That message represents you, and it is your absolute duty to yourself to ensure *it* looks very good, so that *you* look very good.

Before sending an email, take the time to go through it (twice if necessary). Correct the many errors – and there will be many – and only hit send once satisfied that the message is looking good.

WORDS FIRST, ADDRESS SECOND

For many people, the send button is a bit like a period, a full stop. They hastily write their email and click send, only then to think: *"Aw, jeez, maybe I shouldn't have sent that much profanity. Oh well, too late now. Or is it? Maybe I could break into Jim's office, drug his coffee and drop his computer out of the window, then leave a half-empty bottle of Belvedere vodka in his lap, then he'll get fired and THEN he might not see that email."*

To avoid the above scenario, adopt the following simple rule. For every email you create or compose from now on, write the content *first* and once happy – and *only* when once happy – complete the address bar and hit send. This rule gives you a much stronger control over your email communication, and helps to overcome any poor impulses on your part.

REPLY TO ALL?

Probably not! Sheer laziness and a decent amount of "ass-covering" has created a "reply to all" e-society. We feel that, as long as everyone can see what we have said, that's probably a good thing. But this is not the case – our inboxes become full enough without being included in everyone else's minutiae.

Here is one real-world example. Responding to a meeting request recently, a member of my client's team hit reply to all and sent this: *"Hi, Karen, I thought I was going to be able to make this conference call and I still can but I may be several minutes late as I have to take my mom for a few tests."*

More than 30 people on the list now knew that this person's mother might be in need of surgery, hospitalization – or, indeed, further schooling. But quite clearly, only the meeting organizer actually needed to know that she would be a little late to the call.

As humans, we are a curious bunch, so this statement on its own was quite the fascination. How late would she be? What was the nature of these tests? Would she pass? Would she live? Was there no one else around who could drive the mom to the tests?

Believe it or not, it is possible to discover the impact on profitability of that particular "reply to all", through a simple calculation. Thirty people earning on average $80,000 p.a is a total cost to the company over a year of $2.4 million. Divided by the (approximately) 210 working days in the year, this costs the company, $11,428 every day – that is $27 per minute.

So that "reply to all", taking an average of a minute to open, read, laugh at, forward to others for entertainment value and finally delete costs the firm $27. Happening many times a day and multiplied across a national economy in a year, that's literally *millions* of dollars lost on the reply-to-all function.

The same approach must also be adopted for the c.c. function. To copy in or not to copy in, that is the question. More often than not, most other people don't need to know – so before clicking "send", be sure that those who need to see your message are in the loop, and those that don't are left alone!

To save the future, to save us all – it must stop! Okay, maybe that's being a little too dramatic, but this sort of behaviour *is* really annoying. And in the world of soft skills, you want people to be excited, enthused, motivated and encouraged by you – *never* annoyed.

So from this point, before clicking "reply to all" or c.c.-ing loads of extra people, always ask yourself if these people *really* need to see this email. Only send it to those people to whom it is truly relevant and necessary.

IF IN A RAGE, SAVE

How do you feel? Mad? Angry? Indignant? If you feel any of these emotions and you decide to vent your spleen in the form of an email, you must always force yourself to do just one thing. *Save* the message before you send it. While in the throes of your emotional reaction to some outrage or diabolical liberty taken against you, by all means furiously write out and articulate your damaged feelings and extreme threats along with some poisonous bile and dangerous promises. Get it off your chest.

But, at this point, very carefully save it into your drafts folder. Next, go and have a coffee (or Martini, glass of wine, bottle of tequila), or put yourself through a workout at the gym, or play with the kids, dog, other half – anything to occupy your time and allow yourself to cool down and think things through. Sleeping on it is an even better option. After this period of reflection, go back to your message and re-read it. Still happy with the content? Have you fully considered the response it will create and where that might leave you? Still happy? Okay, send it.

Most of the time, however, you will choose to edit this message or indeed delete it altogether. Don't forget: you are the bigger person and your considered response – or lack of response – will have a far more positive impact on a conflict situation than any knee-jerk reaction written and sent in the heat of the moment.

DEMANDING NOTIFICATION

Do not demand a read-response to every single email you send out. People become irritated when someone electronically demands to know if your email has been read or not. *"Adam has requested a confirmation that you read this e-mail. Would you like to respond?"* No, I would not. Many people find this an intrusive and unnecessary step within the email process. I happen to agree.

There is a smarter, more covert method of achieving the same objective, without putting your target to any inconvenience or letting them know what you are up to.

One such solution comes from didtheyreadit.com. Once you sign up for the service, you are able to send emails via their servers. They arrive at your target's inbox with no sign of their hidden spy mechanism or the fact that they have been routed through these servers.

Once your email is opened, you receive a confirmation email from didtheyreadit.com. Better than that, the email tells you how long your email was read for, when it gets opened again and where (geographically) it was viewed.

Cool!! Too cynical and secretive for you? Don't do it then. Be aware, however, that others will!

BREVITY

The whole point of email is that is should be more convenient and often quicker than picking up the phone, and should deal with one or two issues that need to be seen quickly, as part of a larger negotiation or arrangement. Your messages should be brief, concise and succinct. If you find yourself scrolling up for 20 minutes to re-check your message, you've written too much!

FORWARDED JOKES

Your emails have a brand value. This value can rise as well as fall. If you start to forward every half-baked e-joke and monkey video that appears in your inbox, the brand value of your emails will drop as fast as the Dow Jones after a shock interest-rate hike.

Be very selective when deciding to forward humour to your friends, colleagues and clients. Ensure that when someone receives something like this from you it's a rarity and something they will definitely find funny. (However, if you do want to see something funny, do a search on YouTube for "Yorkie tune" …!)

MORE ON BRAND VALUE

Given that each of your messages has a value and a purpose, you should always try to maximize that impact. I try, wherever possible, to add some little nugget of information, link to a story or dash of gossip to ensure that when people read my emails they are getting two things. They are getting a message relevant to whatever our deal is, but they are also getting something tailored specifically to them. For example, I know that one particular colleague is a total airplane obsessive. Every time I email him, I attach a link to a cool new photo of the inside of the Airbus A380 or yet another prototype flying car. Another of my colleagues was having a few health issues so, as well as some information he had requested on my coaching techniques, I sent him a newly published list of specialist doctors that may have been of some use to him. These added gems help me to improve the brand value of my messages. People know that, when they open my email, they are going to get extra. That's something that you can do right away!

Techniquette is the on-line and digital display of your soft skills. Never forget that your continuing job is to show others that you have their interests at heart and that, as a result, you are great to work with. This way you have yet more potential with which to win over friends, colleagues, clients and bosses.

CHAPTER 8

Leveraging your network

> Your network is a big piece of your personal brand –
> after all, you are a product of the people who know
> you, who love you, who work with you and who
> vouch for you. Your network is a living, breathing
> thing and should be nurtured, cared for and
> encouraged to grow. Grow your network and you
> grow yourself and your success.

Growing and nurturing your network in order to leverage its power must become one of your top priorities, and there are a number of ways of doing this.

NURTURING EXISTING CONTACTS

You need to keep yourself on the radar (or sonar!) of your existing and past clients. Just like in all those great war movies, where the captain and members of his anxious crew stare at the green sonar screen as it repeatedly sweeps the ocean ahead. Nothing. Another sweep. Nothing. *"Beep!"* Suddenly, there it is, another sub!

Reminding people that we exist is a little like forcing yourself to pop up on their sonar screens. We may think that we are the most important people in the world, but others tend to forget us after a short while. Getting yourself onto their sonar screens – inboxes, voicemail, desks, cell phones, gyms, golf courses, favourite bars etc – is the perfect way to reintroduce the fact that you are not only alive, but also could well be of some further use.

Naturally, the more you personalize this outreach, the better. No one loves a message that starts, *"Hi everyone"*. It doesn't make them feel special or important. So even if you are creating a mass mailshot, at least try to make it appear directed at a single person. The finest operators of this type of communication will create an individual message for every target.

WHAT IF THERE'S NOTHING TO SAY?

There's always something to say! Simply make the effort to find an item of news, rumour, gossip or interest that is at least, in some way, connected to the person you are connecting with. Generalizing hugely:

- A doctor may like some scientific innovation.

- An executive would probably enjoy some form of top 500 list.

- Most blokes will enjoy a gadget preview.

- Women would perhaps be more interested in fashion, celebrity gossip or niche business news.

- Lawyers want to see legal announcements.

- Political sorts revel in poll numbers.

You can also include cool (and not legally questionable) websites or funny and original on-line video clips – and images. People love images – recent self-taken (gadget or phone) photos are always a good tool, as their very personal and non-business nature almost always encourages a response.

Make them unique to create maximum interest. Sending a photo of you buying some envelopes is clearly not as fascinating as snapping a BlackBerry photo of your wine and canapés at the Paris restaurant where you happen to be enjoying a special lunch. Yes, you're showing off with an implied wink – but, it is more memorable and effective than a standard business note.

What really counts here is simply the discipline of thinking first about what drives your target's interest. The better you know them, the more appropriate will be your offering, and the greater chance your message will generate a response.

So content is easy. All that is required is a little bit of advanced thought and planning. Just keep it short, make sure it's spelled right and always include something of interest or value.

FOLLOWING UP WITH NEW CONTACTS

Remember chapter 4 all about networking? You've just had a great day networking at a conference, or have just met a fabulous person at a party. You've used all your soft skills brilliantly and have made some great new contacts. You've "sold" yourself well and have promised to get in touch with them. Now you've got to follow through and deliver on that promise.

HOW GOOD'S YOUR MEMORY?

Maybe you're fortunate enough to have a photographic memory, and can recall every last thing that all those new people said to you, what they looked like, who they know, what you had in common, and so forth. But for most of us, relying solely on memory to recall all these details can be risky. After several days' relentless networking at an international trade fair you will have met a huge number of new people. Believe me, once you finally step off the plane back home and return to your office, some of these people may have become somewhat mixed up in your mind.

As soon as possible after the event, maybe in the cab on the way home, jot down a few key words and notes to remind you of the details of the individuals you have met –perhaps on the back of their business card. At a very large event such as a trade fair with long aisles and rows of stands, you may be able to do this in between the encounters themselves. The crucial thing is to note down one point of commonality or a topic you chatted about, and what it was you promised them. That way, you can tailor your follow-up around these details.

THE TAILORED FOLLOW-UP

The tailored follow-up – *"It was great to meet someone who shares my passion for jazz …", "I found our chat about the growth of your market share very interesting …"* – is far more effective than a standard anonymous mailshot that you send out to all and sundry (even if you insert the correct name at the top). It shows that you have remembered that particular person and their conversation, and taken the time to treat them as an individual.

Next you simply deliver on your promise: *"You will recall that we talked about you coming in to see our showroom …", "You expressed an interest in finding out more about my consultancy services …"* Suggest that you give them some time to peruse any materials you have enclosed and that you will follow up by phone. That way you are still keeping the door open and have taken one step closer to making this new contact a new client.

THE TELEPHONE FOLLOW-UP

It may be more appropriate that you just follow up by phone straight away. This is, as you know, not the easiest task. Pinning down their availability, actually getting through to them, then holding them for long enough to get your message across is a formidable set of challenges. However, making calls like this is not a million miles away from the concept of releasing people first in a networking situation (see pages 94–7).

Consider for a moment how you feel when approached by a market-research person in the street or at an airport. They approach you with their clipboard and all ask the same question: *"Have you got a minute to answer a few questions?"*

Even though you most likely do have a minute, you will usually (apart from the most generous among you!) claim that you are in a rush and can't stop. You will make a half-hearted apology and offer a weak smile in a bid to stop them utterly condemning you or running after you with an axe.

This fear of being trapped by a clipboard person is very similar to how you feel when someone cold-calls you. The knowledge that you may well be held captive on the phone for some time is an alarming one. In a follow-up phone call, at least you know that you have already established initial contact and interest. Nevertheless, the target may still have more immediate and pressing things to do that day, so the principle still applies: keep it short and sweet.

That said, you do still need to keep the person on the phone long enough for it to count. In order to achieve this, you simply have to do two things:

1. "Pre-end" the call.

2. Pre-empt what they would say.

Pre-ending the call is easy. You start by saying: *"Hi, it's Mark from the Jeffries Corporation. I am just heading out of the office and I haven't got long ..."* By delivering this as an opening statement, you are letting the person on the other end of the line know that this call won't last for hours and that there will be no uncomfortable entrapment.

Pre-empting what they would say is also straightforward. You follow on by saying something like: *"... and I know you are very busy, but I just wanted to let you know ..."* By acknowledging that you already know that they are very busy, they cannot say that they are too busy in order to brush you off, as you just said it. Very clever.

You have bought yourself 20 to 30 seconds of valuable phone time to announce something such as an incoming email or a document that will shortly be on its way. You can also use this call to lay an anchor of return – where you announce that you will call again next week or later in the month, leaving that door wedged open.

Whether on the phone or face to face, before delivering their message, a strategic communicator using powerful soft skills will always consider the other person and what it is they need and want.

FOLLOWING UP THE FOLLOW-UP

What if you don't get a response? Sometimes, people are embarrassed at how much time has passed since they last spoke with you. They were busy, distracted and forgot – for months. Now they feel too ashamed to pick up the phone or to send an email. Make it easy for them by reaching out first and apologizing yourself (even though it is not your fault). This breaks the ice and re-establishes the lines of communication.

GROWING YOUR NETWORK

Look at all the people with whom you already have regular contact. If you have sent an email or placed a call within the last four weeks and you received a reply (which was not a threat to call the police or a request for you to never contact them again), the recipient of your "outreach" is in your current network. Ask yourself whether this list of people has grown in the past month. If not, then it's time to make a bit more effort in this area.

Think of all those hideous invitations that have landed on your desk. You know the sort of thing: this benefit, that gala, this street protest (France only), this convention, that gathering.

If you are being truly honest with yourself, you don't really want to go to any of them. You have other priorities – such as the season finale of *Lost* or a great run in the park, finishing the epic workload already on your desk or meeting your friends for a night out. All good stuff. But these invitations open a door to the great unknown; they are a chance to grow your network. Where possible you should always reply, *"Yes, see you there."* Why? Because you never know who you might meet.

Think about your best clients or your most valuable contacts and how you initially met them or were made aware of their existence. Trace it back further – who connected you to them? You will be amazed at how much of your current business will stem from having met one important person at one dreaded event.

I am a huge believer in the power of the unexpected meeting. Years ago I was hosting a TV show that ended at 2pm and that was it. Occasionally, however, a very cute producer, Sabena, used to beg me to stand in and moderate this lame technology programme. It was recorded in the same studio straight after my live show. I never wanted to do it, as it really *was* lame. And no one ever watched.

On this one cold, dark Tuesday, however, with nothing better to do, the producer won me over (she *was* cute) and persuaded me to stay on and host this half hour dull-fest. I had to interview some guy from the IT firm Oracle. Yawn. It turned out to be a fascinating chat, however, and this guy, Nick Barley, and I hit it off. After the interview ended and the lights were turned off, he invited me to come and host one of his major corporate events.

To cut a long story short – from that one event, working with him and his marketing communications genius Alison Masters, I made a stream of valuable contacts from many different organizations which, to this day, form a solid 50 per cent of my overall income. Those people are now spread across other companies and industries, and all over the world. They have introduced me to others and have helped to generate a fabulous flow of business.

There is no doubt in my mind that that single interview on that one day – that one invitation I nearly turned down – changed a huge amount in terms of my direction, career and success.

HEY, I'M ALREADY MAKING MONEY – DO I NEED NEW CONTACTS?

People often say to me, *"I don't need any more friends"* or *"I am busy enough with what's on my plate without having to worry about making new contacts."* I completely understand this, but be careful: often success itself can be your undoing.

The one thing harder than becoming a success is staying a success. As time goes on and you start to enjoy the fruits of your labour, it's easy to conclude that you have it totally made: loads of great clients, people calling you up all the time and business and cash flow coming along well. It's at this point that you may start to become complacent and find yourself doing less self-marketing, making fewer exploratory calls, spending less time at new events, no longer generating hot innovative ideas and, instead, simply devoting all your time to existing clients.

This is always a mistake. Sure, it costs a lot more to nurture and win a new client than it does to leverage an existing one, but eventually, without a stream of new and fresh clients using your services, you will become reliant on one or two big accounts, which is always a dangerous gamble.

The flow of business that you are enjoying now you probably set up over a year ago. It really does take that much time to mature a contact into a client, and yet more time to turn that average client into a great client. So, fast-forward one year from now – your business flow then will directly correlate with your networking activity right now. It's all a bit like gardening. You prepare the soil, plant your seeds and bulbs, and later in the year the flowers emerge – you get results. Your contacts now are the pretty flowers of tomorrow.

It's down to you to create results for yourself, and that need never goes away. You need to constantly leverage and grow your network – keep planting the seeds in order to pick those flowers.

BUSINESS-CARD ALCHEMY –
TURNING PAPER INTO GOLD!

If you are really organized and you have sorted out all your new contacts into "useful" and "useless", you are ahead of the game. But before you throw all those useless business cards into a nearby furnace, you should first try a bit of "email matchmaking".

That's right, those contacts may be of no value to you, but they could be gold dust to someone else. And if you hook them up like some celebrity matchmaker, you build up big credits from both parties. Think for a minute about who you could connect them to within your fabulous network, and send a "matchmaker" email. You know the sort of thing: *"Hi, it suddenly occurred to me that you both have a lot in common and could probably do some great business together … So, in true e-meeting style, Bob, top TV producer, allow me to introduce Sam, a vet who just happens to have a celebrity pet clinic! Let me know how it goes …"*

Both of the above people are pretty irrelevant to your business as a tax attorney, but, hey, to each other – you never know. If they meet with success, your little act of thoughtfulness earns you some useful business "payback credits". In fact, whether they hook up or not, they will both feel that they owe you something. After all, not only did you think about them, but also you felt that they were both good enough at what they do for you to suggest matching them up.

In the world of soft skills, how you are perceived is hugely important. Here you are branding yourself as a connector of people, a business-minded networker, a friend and someone who doesn't always put themselves first. Cool. I like you already.

YOUR NETWORK – YOUR SALESPEOPLE

We spend our life exposed to advertising – we see its messages, we are enticed by its images and we are bombarded with its relentless impact.

Despite the Madison Avenue millions spent on this modern-day art form, it's often friends, buddies and contacts who will convince us of the need to buy a product. In other words: word of mouth. It's pretty obvious why. We trust the words of someone impartial far more than someone who stands to make some money out of that recommendation.

Simplest example in the world. TV ad. Scene: middle-aged man in suit on car lot, shouting in our direction, clutching granddaughter for emotional impact (nice). *"Hi, I'm Brad Drake, and these are the finest cars your money could buy. This week we are having a sale to beat all sales. That's right ..."* And so his spiel continues.

When you watch this visual "feast", do you (a) drop everything and race down to the car dealership to buy as many of these quality used vehicles as your wife's money will buy? Or (b) think about it for a bit, then completely forget about it? Or (c) scoff at this poor attempt to win you over and wonder what type of loser actually falls for this trash?

Now imagine you are sitting down on a Saturday night with friends at a local restaurant, and one of your closest acquaintances leans forwards and says, *"You won't believe how much money I saved on this car I just bought. Seriously, the dealer can't do his math. I bought such a great car for about two grand less than I should have done."* Now you are interested.

You need a plumber to sort out a leak. Where do you go? AAA Plumbing in the *Yellow Pages,* or ask a friend who they last used and whether they were any good? We trust the word of a friend or contact, as we know they have nothing to gain out of recommending something to us, other than them wanting us to share in something good.

YOUR NETWORK'S NETWORK

Here's where you pull in the favours. For example, you are running a small web-design agency, and the people in your network – your existing clients – know that you are really good. It's time to make use of that goodwill. Seriously, why not?

Often this will work all on its own. People like to share their discoveries and recommendations. If it's not happening, give them a call or send them an email. Mention how you're entering the "next phase of growth" and ask them if they know anyone in their network who could benefit from a cool new-look website with a bunch of innovative features. Add a little incentive, such as, *"Hey, if you hook me up with some business, I'll owe you. Maybe we should set up a little commission structure or head out to that fabulous new restaurant."* Only you can judge how far you can push this recompense idea and what is right to offer, but you should somehow convey the message that you are prepared to recognize this special request for effort from them.

NETWORKING TECHNOLOGY

There is a number of useful social and business networking sites available at the moment including MySpace, Facebook and LinkedIn. As you may know, they give you the chance to cyber-connect with people who are similar to you, or could be useful to you or with whom you could become friends. It is a great way of retaining your presence on the radar screen and ensuring you are part of what is going on.

While the other sites are predominantly social, LinkedIn is dedicated to business. It has an innovative user interface that allows you to spread your connections to the nth degree – theoretically allowing you to make contact with people many positions away from your immediate circle.

At its core, this cyber-networking approach allows you to take advantage of "barriers-down" theory, by encouraging you to use people who are known to both parties to connect new contacts. Simply by showing that you are "LinkedIn" with Kevin might allow you to connect with Meredith. Previously, Meredith may not have even answered your email.

Often, though, people simply collect contacts and never do anything with them. So it pays to be proactive and to reach out occasionally across this cyber network and gently push contacts into remembering your excellent product and how important they are to you.

You can also play the role of "connector" and earn some free "payback credits", simply by spending a bit of time creating some "corporate matchmaker" emails among your cyber contacts.

Use these technologies wisely and with a subtle approach and they will do a lot of the work for you.

Conclusion

Soft skills and strategic communication are a way of life. They represent an approach that is open, generous, adaptive and thoughtful. Yet, at its core, there is a selfish driver: the need to grow your own success and to get ahead of the competition.

In an ironic twist, however, in your bid to do better and tilt the scales in your favour, you will make more friends, grow valuable contacts and create a group of people who will always vouch for you.

You will become a better communicator – a skill that will not only earn you more in the business world, but will lift you in the social world too. Using the ideas in these pages will also raise your positive effect as partner, lover and friend.

As you start to practise the ideas in this book, you will become a sharper observer of people, you will understand their needs faster than your competition and you will engender trust all around you. These finely honed skills will help you in all areas of your life.

Remember, these ideas are presented as a tool kit – it is up to you to decide when and how you use the tools that suit you best.

Use them wisely, use them often and be successful!

To Contact Mark Jeffries

Contact information, further ideas, innovative podcasts and insightful video clips about:

- Advanced presentation coaching
- Strategic media coaching
- Group-pitch and presentation sessions
- The competitive-pitch game
- The keynote speech
- Event hosting and facilitation

– are all available at www.markjeffries.com.

For bookings and more details contact:

UK: +44 (0)20 8421 9256
USA: Meredith Kennedy, Washington Speakers Bureau
          +1 (703) 684-0555 x 1062
Canada: Martin Perelmuter, Speaker's Spotlight
          +1 (416) 345-1559 x 202

Index

Author's Acknowledgements

Those who know me will agree that this book took way, way too long. It was one of those projects that stopped and started, changed, evolved stopped again and then sprinted to completion.

The ideas within are born of the people and stories that have surrounded my life of relentless communication and constant travel.

Every wonderful client who invites me to speak at their meeting or event teaches me something new. Every great speaker who requests my advice and coaching adds to my knowledge. Everyone I meet contributes to my depth of understanding and the (hopefully!) freshness of my inspiration.

So – I thank everyone whose acquaintance I have made. Special mention, in no specific order, to: Alison Masters and Nick Barley, great communicators who saw the potential and started my adventures; Sally Hanson, Jane Baird, Dave Laverty and Sean Reid – smart marketing minds, bringing together perfect teams to create the best events; Martin and Farah Perelmuter who run Canada's finest speaker agency (Speaker's Spotlight) in an innovative, proud and proactive way; Meredith Kennedy whose support and insight brought me into America's leading speaker agency, Washington Speakers Bureau; Michael Holtz without whom the world couldn't travel!

And for their inspiration, enthusiasm, support, love and laughs, Jason T, Petrie H, Richard C, Karen G and Raffi B. And of course – Ollie, Hannah and Spoodles.

I would also like to thank Naomi Waters for her patience, understanding and work in helping to order a wild and ragged collection of thoughts and turn them into this book.